12 Spirits Seducing the Church

DARRELL MCMANUS

12 Spirits Seducing the Church

RevMedia Publishing
P.O. Box 5172
Kingwood, TX 77325
www.revmediapublishing.com

ISBN: 978-1-7345273-6-0
Printed in the United States of America

References

The Bible

AMP: The Amplified Bible; *The Amplified Bible (AMP) Containing the Amplified Old Testament and Containing The Amplified New Testament.* Copyright © 1954, 1958, 1962, 1964, 1965, 1987 by The Lockman Foundation, La Habra, California. All Rights reserved.

MSG: The Message Bible; *THE MESSAGE: The Bible in Contemporary Language* © 2002 by Eugene H. Peterson. All rights reserved.

NKJV: New King James Version®. Copyright © 1982 by Thomas Nelson, Inc. Used by permission. All rights reserved.

Darby: The Darby Version of the Bible. (Public Domain)

Beware of Seducing Spirits by Mark T. Barclay, M. Barclay Ministries, 1995.

Confronting Jezebel by Steve Sampson, Sovereign World, 1996, 2003

Introduction

In this course of study, we will be dealing with the two words Paul used to describe the subject of this book, "seducing spirits":

In 1 Tim. 4:1, we read, "BUT THE [Holy] Spirit distinctly and expressly declares that in latter times some will turn away from the faith, giving attention to deluding and seducing spirits and doctrines that demons teach, (AMP)."

This is a study of specific groups of seducing spirits sent by Satan to target anointed homes, churches, and ministries to try to utterly destroy them. Since these demons worked through certain people mentioned in scripture, I have named them accordingly. 1 Tim 4:6 says that anyone who is willing to deal with seducing spirits is considered to be a worthy steward and a good minister of Jesus Christ. That is my heart's desire and that is why I have written this book.

Before we get into the specifics of this crucial study, let's take a look at an important scripture that will help us set the stage.

Jude 1-21

I, Jude, am a slave to Jesus Christ and brother to James, writing to those loved by God the Father, called and kept safe by Jesus Christ. 2 Relax, everything's going to be all right; rest, everything's coming together; open your hearts, love is on the way!

Fight with All You Have in You

3 Dear friends, I've dropped everything to write you about
this life of salvation that we have in common. I have to
write insisting — begging! — that you fight with everything
you have in you for this faith entrusted to us as a gift to
guard and cherish.
4 What has happened is that some people have infiltrated our
ranks (our Scriptures warned us this would happen), who
beneath their pious skin are shameless scoundrels. Their
design is to replace the sheer grace of our God with sheer
license — which means doing away with Jesus Christ, our
one and only Master.

Lost Stars in Outer Space

5 I'm laying this out as clearly as I can, even though you once
knew all this well enough and shouldn't need reminding.
Here it is in brief: The Master saved a people out of the
land of Egypt. Later he destroyed those who defected. 6
And you know the story of the angels who didn't stick to
their post, abandoning it for other, darker missions. But
they are now chained and jailed in a black hole until the
great Judgment Day.
7 Sodom and Gomorrah, which went to sexual rack and
ruin along with the surrounding cities that acted just like
them, are another example. Burning and burning and never
burning up, they serve still as a stock warning. 8 This is
exactly the same program of these latest infiltrators: dirty
sex, rule and rulers thrown out, glory dragged in the mud.
9 The Archangel Michael, who went to the mat with the Devil

*as they fought over the body of Moses, wouldn't have dared
level him with a blasphemous curse, but said simply, "No you
don't. God will take care of you!" 10 But these people sneer
at anything they can't understand, and by doing whatever
they feel like doing — living by animal instinct only — they
participate in their own destruction. 11 I'm fed up with
them! They've gone down Cain's road; they've been sucked
into Balaam's error by greed; they're canceled out in Korah's
rebellion. 12 These people are warts on your love feasts as
you worship and eat together. They're giving you a black eye
carousing shamelessly, grabbing anything that isn't nailed
down. They're puffs of smoke pushed by gusts of wind; late
autumn trees stripped clean of leaf and fruit, doubly dead,
pulled up by the roots;*
*13 wild ocean waves leaving nothing on the beach but the
foam of their shame;*

Lost stars in outer space on their way to the black hole.

*14 Enoch, the seventh after Adam, prophesied of them:
"Look! The Master comes with thousands of holy angels 15
to bring judgment against them all, convicting each person
of every defiling act of shameless sacrilege, of every dirty
word they have spewed of their pious filth." 16 These are
the "grumpers," the bellyachers, grabbing for the biggest
piece of the pie, talking big, saying anything they think will
get them ahead.*
*17 But remember, dear friends, that the apostles of our Master,
Jesus Christ, told us this would happen: 18 "In the last days
there will be people who don't take these things seriously*

> *anymore. They'll treat them like a joke, and make a religion of their own whims and lusts." 19 These are the ones who split churches, thinking only of themselves. There's nothing to them, no sign of the Spirit!*
> *20 But you, dear friends, carefully build yourselves up in this most holy faith by praying in the Holy Spirit, 21 staying right at the center of God's love, keeping your arms open and outstretched, ready for the mercy of our Master, Jesus Christ. This is the unending life, the real life!* MSG

There are a multitude of other scriptures that back this up:

2 Peter 2 has some important warnings about the clever ways in which lying, deceiving spirits worm their way into churches, ministries and Christian households, in order to poison the minds of true believers and wreak havoc in their midst. They pervert the Way of Truth, "giving it a bad name" (2 Pet. 2:2) The Scriptures impart stark warnings as to the end result of those who have given ear to these seducing spirits: the fate of the fallen angels; the flood of Noah's day; the destruction of Sodom and Gomorrah; the folly of Balaam, to name a few.

Those who are controlled by these "seducing spirits" are likened to brute beasts—"predators on the prowl" (2 Pet 2:12) They are called "dried-up fountains" and "loudmouths, full of hot air" (2 Pet 2:17,18) But just as a hot-air balloon can be a very dangerous item if the gas gets ignited, so, too, can these "hot-air-filled loudmouths" be destructive if their lies and deceitfulness are allowed to ignite and spread in your church, your ministry, or your home. Take heed!

This passage of scripture ends with a grave warning to all who are drawn away by "seducing spirits": "If they've escaped from the slum of sin by experiencing our Master and Savior, Jesus Christ, and then slid back into that same old life again, they're worse than if they had never left. 21 Better not to have started out on the straight road to God than to start out and then turn back, repudiating the experience and the holy command. 22 They prove the point of the proverbs, "A dog goes back to its own vomit," and, "A scrubbed-up pig heads for the mud (2 Pet.2:20-22, MSG)."

We need to stand guard against these insidious attempts by the Enemy, who is a "liar and the father of lies" (John 8:44), who goes about like a hungry lion, looking for prey to devour (1 Pet. 5:8) Now this doesn't mean that we are to be paranoid—seeing Satan behind every bush and tree; but we do have to be vigilant, understanding that, if there's even the slightest open door, that old serpent will find a way to slither in.

One of the ways that the devil gets to us is through our emotions (the heart-door), especially in the areas of pride and jealousy.

James 3:14-16

14 But if you have bitter jealousy (envy) and contention (rivalry, selfish ambition) in your hearts, do not pride yourselves on it and thus be in defiance of and false to the Truth.
15 This [superficial] wisdom is not such as comes down from above, but is earthly, unspiritual (animal), even devilish (demoniacal).
16 For wherever there is jealousy (envy) and contention (rivalry and selfish ambition), there will also be confusion

(unrest, disharmony, rebellion) and all sorts of evil and vile practices. —AMP

No wonder that the Word tells us to put on the *"breastplate of righteousness" (Eph. 6:14):* the breastplate covers and protects the heart!

As this scripture clearly indicates, we need to beware of jealousy and the contention spawned from pride. The "seducing spirits" love those two human emotions, because they are open doorways into the heart and soul! These seducing spirits often work through people, who, like wolves in sheep's clothing, enter the flock in such good disguises that they often go unnoticed—until they begin to stir up contention and strife.

Paul, in his letter to Titus, calls such demonically-motivated individuals as "corrupt and unbelieving," and says that their "very minds and consciences are defiled and polluted. (Titus 1:15)." He goes on to warn Titus that such people act like they know God—they might be very good at "talking the talk"—but inwardly they deny God and are disloyal and rebellious. Paul says that they are incapable of good work of any kind. (Titus 1:16)

Let's look at another important scripture:

2 Timothy 3:1-5

1 BUT UNDERSTAND this, that in the last days will come (set in) perilous times of great stress and trouble [hard to deal with and hard to bear].

2 For people will be lovers of self and [utterly] self-centered,

lovers of money and aroused by an inordinate [greedy] desire for wealth, proud and arrogant and contemptuous boasters. They will be abusive (blasphemous, scoffing), disobedient to parents, ungrateful, unholy and profane.
3 [They will be] without natural [human] affection (callous and inhuman), relentless (admitting of no truce or appeasement); [they will be] slanderers (false accusers, troublemakers), intemperate and loose in morals and conduct, uncontrolled and fierce, haters of good.
4 [They will be] treacherous [betrayers], rash, [and] inflated with self-conceit. [They will be] lovers of sensual pleasures and vain amusements more than and rather than lovers of God.
5 For [although] they hold a form of piety (true religion), they deny and reject and are strangers to the power of it [their conduct belies the genuineness of their profession]. Avoid [all] such people [turn away from them]. —AMP

Talk about an indictment! Paul really didn't pull any punches here! He wanted to make sure that Timothy, his spiritual son, was well-aware of the manner in which seducing spirits affect and control the people who allow them entrance into their lives; and how dangerous it is to let such people operate within their congregations. Paul admonishes Timothy to steer clear of them and have nothing whatsoever to do with such troublemakers.

Paul goes on in 2 Timothy 3 to explain how the seducing spirits motivate their human hosts to lead others astray—especially those who are weak in the faith, and thus, easily manipulated and persuaded.

These seducing spirits are so dangerous because they are very clever and highly skilled in the "art of deception."

We certainly live in a day in which great deception has crept into the church. It is no longer popular to use the word sin in a number of camps. The cross has been removed from many churches because it is offensive. Many no longer submit to the spiritual authority God has set in place. Lawlessness seems to permeate the very atmosphere we live in. Many churches and ministries are sitting on a proverbial time bomb. Undercurrents of rebellion have successfully wound their way into the foundational fabric of seemingly successful ministries and churches.

These time bombs are sure to go off without warning unless they are biblically identified and exposed. In this course of study, we have identified twelve entities with twelve corresponding names found in the scripture.

There are characteristics and tests for each of these twelve. I strongly suggest that every individual, ministry, church, ministerial staff member, and church staff member study and take the test for each of these twelve seducing spirits to make sure none of these demon forces are working in their lives.

1. The Korah Spirit

"The Rebellious and Insolent Spirit"

In Numbers, chapter 16, we read the account of Korah, the great-grandson of Levi, who, with a handful of Reubenites, rebelled against the God-ordained authority of Moses as leader of Israel. Korah was jealous of Moses's position and that jealousy provided an open door through which a seducing spirit gained entrance into his life. This spirit prodded Korah into open defiance of Moses. He began to murmur behind Moses's back, stirring up contention among the Israelites and eventually persuading a number of Reubenites and 250 leaders among the tribes of Israel to side with him against Moses:

"They came as a group and confronted Moses and Aaron, saying, 'You've overstepped yourself. This entire community is holy and God is in their midst. So why do you act like you're running the whole show?' (Numbers 16:3, MSG)"

Now the 250 men, whom Korah (motivated by the seducing spirit) stirred up against Moses were not just anybody: They were "prominent men with positions in the Council" (verse 2). This seducing spirit meant to take Moses down!

What did Moses do? Did he run, quaking in his sandals? Did he try to appease this crowd of men by bargaining with them? NO! Moses prayed! The scripture tells us that he *"threw himself facedown on the ground" (Num. 16:4):* He fell prostrate before the Lord! Then he told Korah and his band of malcontents what to do:

> *"Tomorrow, take censers. In the presence of God, put fire in them and then incense. Then we'll see who is holy, see whom God chooses. Sons of Levi, you've overstepped yourselves! (Num. 16:7, MSG)"*
>
> *The Levites, who had been given by God the honorable—and important—position of service "in the ministries of The Dwelling of God" (Num. 16:8) and of leading the congregation into the presence of the Almighty, wanted more. They wanted the priesthood, as well! (Num. 16:10)*
>
> *Moses cut to the core of the matter when he declared, "It's God you've ganged up against, not us (Num.16:11, MSG)."*

Moses didn't get angry...and he didn't get offended. He knew, through the Spirit of God, who was behind this rebellion; and he had faith that God Himself would reveal the Truth and vindicate His servants.

The next day, when Korah came with his 250 allies, all equipped with their censers full of incense to present before the Lord, God told Moses,

> *"Separate yourselves from this congregation so that I can finish them off and be done with them (Num. 16:21, MSG)."*

God meant business! He was about to wipe out ALL the Israelites. But Moses and Aaron fell upon the ground and pleaded for their people to be spared. They knew that Korah and his handful of men were the ones who had stirred up discontent among the people:

> *"O God, God of everything living, when one man sins*

are you going to take it out on the whole community? (Num.16:22, MSG) "

God noted the mercy and compassion of His servant, Moses, so He relented, but judgment had to be rendered. So God instructed Moses to tell the congregation of Israel to stay far away from the tents of Korah, Dathan, and Abiram—the three men who had originally stirred up the people against Moses and Aaron. As soon as this command was carried out, the ground opened up and swallowed Korah, Dathan, Abiram and their entire households—even their animals.

And then, the 250 Council members who had sided with Korah and his men were consumed by fire!

Now, you would think that this would have settled the matter once and for all; but the very next day, the people of Israel began to gripe and complain against Moses and Aaron: *"You have killed God's people (Num. 16:41, MSG)!"*

Can you see the effect those seducing spirits had upon Israel? Even when God brought judgment upon the instigators of the contention and strife that had been roiling like muddy waters throughout the congregation, they still insisted upon blaming Moses and Aaron... and they still continued to gripe and complain!

So, the Lord brought one final, decisive judgment upon them: He sent a plague in their midst!

"Back away from this congregation so that I can do away with them this very minute." They threw themselves facedown

> *on the ground. Moses said to Aaron, "Take your censer and fill it with incense, along with fire from the Altar. Get to the congregation as fast as you can: make atonement for them. Anger is pouring out from God — the plague has started (Num. 16:45,46, MSG)!"*

Moses quickly interceded for Israel once again and sent Aaron, censer-in-hand, into the midst of the people. For the sake of his righteous servants, God stopped the plague, but not before 14,700 people had died from it.

Whenever I read this account, I am reminded how little things have changed throughout the thousands of years of human history. People continue to allow Satan to motivate them, rather than the Creator.

Many independent and denominational churches today have people in their midst like Korah and his men. It is so prevalent, it makes one wonder if those churches read this Korah account and patterned their systems after it. I'm issuing a warning. Don't get caught up in it!

Verse two uses the word rebelled; another translation uses the word insolent. To rebel is to refuse to obey rules or authority, to rise in arms against the government. To be insolent is to be boldly rude or disrespectful, contemptuously impertinent and insulting. Impertinent means to be intrusive and uncivil. The phrase "to add insult to injury" fits here.

Why is it, when people have unresolved personal problems,

they have to blame someone in spiritual authority over them? Rebellious, insolent people need to take responsibility for their own unhappiness and actions.

Remember who Korah got to side with him. It wasn't the poor, little weak lambs, but 250 well-known church leaders. Not only that, they were also appointees and members of the council.

Just like today, all it takes is one insolent and mouthy Korah to pollute the minds and hearts of other leaders. Sheep do not do such things. You must be very selective as to whom you appoint as leaders; they can turn on you in a moment.

Make the decision not to be a carnal garbage collector. Do not deliver garbage! And do not accept a garbage delivery. Instead become a garbage buster.

Ask yourself this question: How do your friends really see you? Do they say kind, things about you and laud your Christ-like manner, or do they refer to you as Sister Smut or Brother Big Mouth? Are you known in the ministry in which you serve as a peacemaker or a rebel? Do you have the reputation for being upright and holy, or troublesome and devilish?

Korah and his followers told Moses he had gone too far this time. They claimed he had elevated himself above the Lord's assembly. This same mindset is permeating many churches today. "Who made you my boss, Preacher?" "What makes your decisions always right?" "Why should you have the final say?" "You should submit to us. We outnumber you, and we are the ones who are holy."

Korah and his followers wanted to overthrow God's chosen servant, Moses, and strip him of his position as spiritual leader of Israel. But only Moses had the burning bush experience; God chose him, not man. Man can't fire whom God hires. Korah and his gang wanted Moses out of the picture, so they could have the final say in all the decision-making. This is the way it works: One man stirs up other leaders against what they call a "one-man-show." Then, after they get rid of the so-called "one-man-show," the instigator of the coup announces that the team has been disbanded and he, himself, is now the leader.

The truth of the matter—as in the case of Korah and his men—is that these people, even though they held positions as leaders, were not qualified for those ministry offices. Even if they had certain qualifications, the fact remains that they were not assigned to it. All of us as Christians will be judged from our assignment book in Psalms 139:16.

> *"Your eyes saw my unformed substance, and in Your book all the days [of my life] were written before ever they took shape, when as yet there was none of them."* (AMP)

All that God wants us to accomplish has been recorded in each of our assignment books. It would prevent many ministry errors and failures if we would take a moment and ask the Lord to download our assignment books into our spirits and guide us daily according to our individual assignments, so that we can accomplish His will for our lives each and every day. Even when it is time to move on from one church or ministry to another, there is a right and wrong way to do it. When someone leaves a church or ministry, it should follow the Acts chapter 13 pattern:

> *"Now in the church that was at Antioch there were certain prophets and teachers: Barnabas, Simeon who was called Niger, Lucius of Cyrene, Manaen who had been brought up with Herod the tetrarch, and Saul. As they ministered to the Lord and fasted, the Holy Spirit said, "Now separate to Me Barnabas and Saul for the work to which I have called them." Then, having fasted and prayed and laid hands on them, they sent them away.*

Preaching in Cyprus

> *So, being sent out by the Holy Spirit, they went down to Seleucia, and from there they sailed to Cyprus. And when they arrived in Salamis, they preached the word of God in the synagogues of the Jews. They also had John as their assistant." (NKJV)*

Unfortunately, rather than following this scriptural pattern, many times people leave covertly, without a word, not even bothering to consult their pastor or leader. Some go home, others start their own church or ministry, some dive into a life of sin, while others follow the Korah Spirit.

There are people all over this world, who operate under the influence of satanic spirits in their vendetta against the five-fold ministry of apostles, prophets, evangelists, pastors and teachers. What a sad commentary to be known as one who defamed others and spewed vomit upon them! What an epitaph to leave on one's tombstone: "My mission in life was to persecute God's anointed and appointed."

Don't be a Korah!

A. Characteristics of the Korah Spirit:

1. You will not like the minister's style of leadership.
2. You will believe the congregation is holy, but the leader is shaky.
3. You will not trust the man or woman of God and may even suspect him or her of stealing money.
4. You will yield to a controlling spirit and will want to be a board member or in another leadership position, so you can change things you do not like.
5. You will believe that your job is to watch, inspect, and judge the minister, instead of obeying God's Word and helping the people.
6. You will be the instigator of banding people together against the man or woman of God in home meetings, or you will initiate a petition of impeachment.
7. You will move out of secret meetings and start to openly challenge your spiritual leaders.
8. You will declare the anointing is gone and will proclaim things like cult or unfair.
9. You will eventually remove yourself from the church or ministry because your scheme has failed; you will leave because of your pride.

B. The Korah Test for Leaders:

1. Do I have a hard time with the person over me in the Lord?
2. Do I feel that he or she has unfair expectations of me to perform in spiritual matters?

3. Do I often want to meet with someone else and talk against the apostle, prophet, evangelist, pastor or teacher I serve in the ministry?
4. Do I feel that 250 other parishioners and I are better at leadership than just one person?
5. Am I often dissatisfied with being in the ministry of helps, and do I go on campaigns to try to put myself into the pulpit ministry?
6. Do I often declare that the one under whom I serve is too hard or abrasive in dealing with the congregation?
7. Do I shout cult, unfair, too strong, or too much control concerning my spiritual leader?
8. Do I often find the need to tell other people what I feel and see just to get it off my chest, even if what I am saying is gossip or murmuring?

THE KORAH TEST FOR RELATIONSHIPS:

1. Do I have a hard time with family members, friends or the people with whom I work?
2. Do I feel that people have unfair expectations of me to perform at home, at work or at play?
3. Do I often want to meet with someone else to talk against my spouse, in-laws, parents, other relatives, friends or co-workers?
4. Do I often declare that my boss is too hard or abrasive when dealing with those under him/her (especially when it comes to me)?
5. Do I often feel the need to tell other people what I feel or see at home or at work, just to get it off my chest, even if what I

say is gossip or murmuring?

If you answered yes to any of the above, you need to sincerely repent and turn completely to the Lord for total restoration!

Pray this prayer:

Father, I come to you in the name of Jesus. I ask you to forgive me for yielding myself to a Korah spirit. Forgive me for tolerating and being sympathetic to Korah's ways. Purify my heart, Lord. Remove every wicked way from my life. Help me to boldly stand against this destructive thought process. Help me to receive the saving of my soul man (mind, will, and emotions) in this area according to 1 Peter 1:9, which is the end or goal of my faith. Even more specifically, help me receive the saving and delivering of my mind (thoughts, feelings, and affections) in this area. Without reservation, I bind and renounce the Spirit of Korah. I pull down this stronghold in my life and bring every thought into captivity to the obedience of Christ. You have been found out, Korah, and will no longer work in my life. Let me walk in Your Light, Lord, and give me discerning eyes and ears to recognize and expose any darkness in my path. I am totally free, and will remain free. I give you praise for this, Father, in Jesus' name, Amen.

2. The Jezebel Spirit

The Spirit of Hatred, Seduction, Intimidation and Control

You all know the story about Jezebel, the wife of King Ahab, and how she tried to kill the prophets of God. Obadiah had to hide a hundred of them away in two caves to protect them from this evil woman. Elijah the Prophet had been a bit of a pariah at the time, hunted far and wide by Ahab's men. He had incurred the wrath of Jezebel when he challenged the 450 prophets of Baal to a test: Come meet me tomorrow on Mount Carmel: Bring along two bulls, and the children of Israel as a witness. You prophets of Baal take one bull and cut it into pieces and lay the pieces upon your altar. I will do the same with mine. Then you begin to call upon the names of your gods, and I will call upon the name of the Lord. The god who brings fire upon his altar first, he is the true God!

Of course, they all agreed, and the meeting took place as Elijah had commanded. The prophets of Baal were so sure that their god would prevail! But after calling upon Baal all morning to no avail, Elijah began to make sport of them, saying, "Hey, maybe your god's off meditating somewhere and can't hear you...Or maybe he's taken a trip to a far place...Or, perhaps, he's asleep. So maybe you should just shout more loudly and wake him up!"

Now that didn't sit well with the prophets of Baal and they began to jump up and down and cry aloud and cut themselves till blood was everywhere. All afternoon and evening they did this—and still no reply!

Finally, Elijah directed the people to pay heed to him as he built his altar and had water poured over the offering until it was totally drenched. Then he called upon the name of the Lord:

"Lord God of Abraham, Isaac, and Israel, let it be known this day that You are God in Israel and I am Your servant, and that I have done all these things at Your word. 37 Hear me, O Lord, hear me, that this people may know that You are the Lord God, and that You have turned their hearts back to You again (1 Kings 18: 36.37, NKJV)

Immediately, fire fell from heaven and burnt up everything—even the stones of the altar and the water that had run off the altar into the surrounding trench! All of the children of Israel fell on their faces, proclaiming,

"The Lord, He is God! The Lord, He is God!" (I Kings 18:39, NKJV)

Then Elijah commanded that the 450 prophets of Baal be seized, and they were taken to the brook Kishon and put to death there.

When Jezebel learned of this, she became enraged and sought to kill Elijah. We read of this in 1 Kings 19: 1, 2:

"Ah

ab reported to Jezebel everything that Elijah had done, including the massacre of the prophets. Jezebel immediately sent a messenger to Elijah with her threat: 'The gods will get you for this and I'll get even with you! By this time tomorrow you'll be as dead as any one of those prophets (MSG).' "

The Spirit of Jezebel is a destroying spirit: It will seek to destroy your ministry, your testimony, your integrity, your marriage—whatever it can lay waste to! If it does not get what it wants, it will attempt to hunt you down and take you out!

Remember the story of Naboth the Jezreelite, in 1 Kings, chapter 21. Naboth had a choice vineyard near Ahab's palace in Samaria... and Ahab wanted it. He went to Naboth and offered him "a deal":

> *"Ahab said to Naboth, Give me your vineyard, that I may have it for a garden of herbs, because it is near my house. I will give you a better vineyard for it or, if you prefer, I will give you its worth in money (1 Kings 21: 2, AMP). "*

Ahab must've thought he had made Naboth "an offer he couldn't refuse." So imagine his surprise when Naboth said,

> *"The Lord forbid that I should give the inheritance of my fathers to you (1 Kings 21: 3, AMP)."*

King Ahab got all sulky and went home and lay in his bed, like a spoiled child who had not gotten his way. He even refused to eat! When Jezebel asked Ahab what was wrong, he told her of Naboth's refusal to sell him his field. Jezebel replied,

> *"Do you not govern Israel? Arise, eat food, and let your heart be happy. I will give you the vineyard of Naboth the Jezreelite (1 Kings 21:7, AMP)."*

Then this wicked queen devised a plan to destroy Naboth:

> *"So she wrote letters in Ahab's name and sealed them with his seal and sent them to the elders and nobles who dwelt with Naboth in his city. And in the letters she said, Proclaim*

a fast and set Naboth up high among the people. And set two men, base fellows, before him, and let them bear witness against him, saying, You cursed and renounced God and the king. Then carry him out and stone him to death. (1 Kings 21: 8-10, AMP)"

And that is exactly what they did! Do you see how dangerously manipulative this spirit is? It will wreak total havoc in your life, if you let it. It will stir up others against you to destroy you! Or it will stir you up against someone else. Beware!

When the Lord told the prophet Elijah what Jezebel had done, he went to meet Ahab in Naboth's vineyard. God gave Elijah some harsh words to impart to the king:

"In the place where dogs licked the blood of Naboth shall dogs lick your blood, even yours (1 Kings 21:19, AMP)." This got Ahab's attention. But the Lord wasn't through with Ahab yet:

"See, I will bring evil on you and utterly sweep away and cut off from Ahab every male, bond and free,

And will make your household like that of Jeroboam son of Nebat and like the household of Baasha son of Ahijah, for the provocation with which you have provoked Me to anger and made Israel to sin.

Also the Lord said of Jezebel: The dogs shall eat Jezebel by the wall of Jezreel.

Any belonging to Ahab who dies in the city the dogs shall eat, and any who dies in the field the birds of the air shall eat (1 Kings 21:21-24, AMP)." [see 1 Kings 14:11; 16:4.]

Now that REALLY got Ahab's attention. The scriptures tell us that

Ahab tore his clothes, put on sackcloth, lay on his face and fasted before the Lord. His act of contrition moved the Lord to defer the evil in his lifetime. But judgment came upon his children and his children's children.

What had gone so wrong in King Ahab's life? He listened to Jezebel and let her control him:

"For there was no one who sold himself to do evil in the sight of the Lord as did Ahab, incited by his wife Jezebel (1 Kings 21:25, AMP)."

The very same Jezebel Spirit that brought ruin to the house of Ahab is alive and well today, operating in and through those, who like Ahab, are weak and easily manipulated. This spirit not only inspires fleshly sins, but spiritual ones, as well:

In Revelation 2:20-23, we read:

"But I have this against you: that you tolerate the woman Jezebel, who calls herself a prophetess [claiming to be inspired], and who is teaching and leading astray my servants and beguiling them into practicing sexual vice and eating food sacrificed to idols. [1 Kings 16:31; 2 Kings 9:22,30.]

I gave her time to repent, but she has no desire to repent of her immorality [symbolic of idolatry] and refuses to do so.

Take note: I will throw her on a bed [of anguish], and those who commit adultery with her [her paramours] I will bring down to pressing distress and severe affliction, unless they turn away their minds from conduct [such as] hers and repent of their doings.

And I will strike her children (her proper followers) dead

> *[thoroughly exterminating them]. And all the assemblies (churches) shall recognize and understand that I am He Who searches minds (the thoughts, feelings, and purposes) and the [inmost] hearts, and I will give to each of you [the reward for what you have done] as your work deserves (AMP)." [Ps 62:12; Jer 17:10.]*

Jezebel is a very destructive spirit at work in our present society. Although this spirit primarily affects women, it can work through men as well. The thing that sets this spirit apart from the other eleven is the need for an Ahab or an enabler.

This spirit has destroyed many marriages and ministries.

In a marriage, if the husband is set on committing ungodly acts of control, and allowed to freely do so, the husband is the Jezebel and the wife is the enabler or the Ahab. On the other hand, if the wife is set on committing ungodly acts of control, and allowed to freely do so, the wife is the Jezebel and the husband is the enabler or the Ahab.

Jezebels push for control at all cost, wherever they are allowed to operate.

A. Characteristics of the Jezebel Spirit:

1. Primarily affects women.
2. Requires an Ahab in order to operate.
3. Tries to usurp ministerial authority.
4. Will scheme and cheat to get ahead.
5. Is jealous of the prophets, their popularity, their gifts, as

well as their anointing.

6. Is completely self-centered, following after his/her own desires.
7. Is never at peace with God's leaders; Jezebel is constantly wrestling with and speaking against God's leaders.
8. Often has a miserable marriage.
9. Loves to feed on weaker people.
10. Will give personal prophecies to try to gain superiority over others.
11. Is not teachable, but a very vocal know-it-all. In response to any authority, imparting knowledge on a given subject, this person will often say, "I know all about that."
12. Hangs around the prophetic.
13. Tries to weave into intercessory prayer meetings.
14. Has exalted himself/herself above all authority in the church, and therefore believes his/her role is to examine everyone else's activities and to pass judgment on them.
15. Hates and despises strong male leadership.
16. Feeds on strife.
17. Is always in the middle of, or connected in some way to, any strife-filled situation.
18. Will appear friendly and personable to your face, but will rip you apart to others behind your back.
19. Always carries and promotes another vision that is contrary to the head of any ministry.
20. Will cause a scene when challenged.

21. Must be dealt with in the spirit and confronted head-on, if necessary.
22. Will never admit to being wrong.
23. Uses knowledge or information you don't have, in order to control you.
24. Often changes the subject in order to stay in control of conversations.
25. Quick to volunteer for a project in order to control that project.
26. Is ruled by a lying spirit. Jezebel lies so well she believes her own lies.
27. Will isolate someone who disagrees with him or her by ignoring that person.
28. Is a nonstop talker.
29. Is ungrateful.
30. Seldom gives anyone credit for anything.
31. When confronted, this person will spiritualize the situation to take the focus off himself/herself and put it onto God.
32. Will never take the side of the one in spiritual authority.
33. Will express or imply disapproval of those under his/her influence to maintain control. This can be readily observed in marriages, ministries and work places.
34. Likes to give gifts to manipulate others.
35. Allows no one to speak into his or her life.
36. Is religious, a church goer.
37. Is a very motivated individual, but for personal gain.

38. Can hide for a period of time, but not indefinitely.
39. Will catch you off guard.
40. Will demand attention.
41. Sows discord among the brethren.
42. Constantly seeks revenge.
43. Will call the one who confronts him/her a Jezebel.
44. Is an information gatherer.
45. Will espouse a greater testimony or story than anyone else to always appear to be more spiritual.
46. Is very pushy in an effort to accomplish his or her agenda.
47. Always seeks revenge whenever crossed.
48. Must have the last say.
49. Always strives to come out smelling like a rose in any given situation.

B. Three-fold Judgment That Will Come if She Fails to Repent According to Revelation 2:22-23:

1. Cast Jezebel into a bed of sickness.
2. Bring tribulation upon everyone who commits adultery with her. (There are two types of adultery in scripture: spiritual and physical.)
3. Kill Jezebel's children with death.
4. C. The Jezebel Test for Leaders:
5. Do I quite often desire to shut the preacher's mouth?
6. Do I struggle with gifts and prophecies that I don't deliver?

7. Am I always trying to dominate and overpower my pastor and ministry co-workers?
8. Do I often switch from love to hate or from support to opposition in my relationship with my pastor or the one over me in the Lord?
9. Do I become bitter, hurt, or angry because I personally can't be close, intimate friends with my spiritual leader?
10. Am I easily offended when I am corrected and, because of that, strike out against the leadership?
11. Do I perceive myself as one who is out to gain money, prestige, position, or popularity?
12. Do I require an enabler to accomplish the things I want to achieve?
13. Is my agenda more important than everyone else's?
14. Do I have to be in charge of prayer meetings?
15. Do I give gifts so the recipient will feel obligated to do something in return for me?
16. Do I despise the office of the prophet?

The Jezebel Test for Relationships:

1. Do I often desire to shut my wife's/husband's, friend's, or boss's mouth?
2. Am I always trying to dominate and overpower my husband, wife, boss or friends?
3. Do I often switch from love to hate or from support to opposition in my relationship with my spouse, family members, friends or boss?

4. Do I become bitter, hurt, or angry because I cannot personally be close, intimate friends with my boss?
5. Do I get easily offended when my spouse, family member, friend or boss corrects me, and because of that, do I strike out at the person bringing the correction?
6. Do I see myself as the one who is out to gain money, prestige, position or popularity?
7. Do I require an enabler to accomplish the things I want to achieve?
8. Is my agenda more important than my family or my job?
9. Do I have to be in charge at home, at work or at play?
10. Do I give gifts to family members, friends or co-workers, so that they will feel obligated to do something in return for me?
11. Do I despise my boss?

If you answered yes to any of the above, you need to sincerely repent and turn completely to the Lord for total restoration!

Pray this prayer:

Father, I come to you in the name of Jesus. I ask you to forgive me for yielding myself to a Jezebel spirit. Forgive me for tolerating and being sympathetic to Jezebel's ways. Purify my heart, Lord. Remove every wicked way from my life. Help me to boldly stand against this destructive thought process. Help me to receive the saving of my soul man (mind, will, and emotions) in this area according to 1 Peter 1:9, which is the end or goal of my faith. Even more specifically, help me receive the saving and delivering of my mind (thoughts, feelings, and affections) in this area. Without reservation, I bind and renounce the Spirit of Jezebel. I pull down this stronghold in my life and bring every thought into captivity to the obedience of Christ. You have been found out, Jezebel, and will no longer work in my life. Let me walk in Your Light, Lord, and give me discerning eyes and ears to recognize and expose any darkness in my path. I am totally free, and will remain free. I give you praise for this, Father, in Jesus' name, Amen.

Before we go to spirit number three, there are some things we need to look at. All twelve of these spirits are extremely dangerous. They are ever waiting for you to make a false step to bring you and your ministry down. Don't jump in a direction, just because it is the right direction; timing is everything. You can be at the right place at the wrong time and miss it. You can be at the wrong place at the right time and miss it. Following God will always cause you to be at the right place at the right time.

God commanded the ravens to feed Elijah the prophet at Cherith brook at a specific time. There was nowhere else on planet earth that Elijah could have gone at that time to receive God's provision. It was not a place teeming with people, ready to meet his needs. He had to rely solely upon the Lord. Some of you would have a problem with such an instruction. But remember: There are some places in God that only you can go. Are you prepared to humble yourselves and follow God's leading?

Notice the circumstance through which Elijah saw that God's provision would have become a death trap had he stayed put. The brook that was flowing so well dried up! Zarephath then became the place called "there" in Elijah's life and ministry. Just as God had commanded the ravens to feed Elijah at the "there" called "the brook Cherith," the "there" then changed to "Zarephath." God had commanded a widow woman to feed Elijah at that specific time.

If you are following what God is doing, rather than following God Himself, or if you are a prophecy or miracle seeker, it can cost you your life and ministry. That's right; it can put you in an early grave. Do you want to die early? If your answer is "no," then, stop following what is happening at the moment and follow Yahweh, The "I Am," The One Who Is, The Self-Existent One.

You must know God intimately and personally; your life and ministry depends on it. Compare yourself to no one! Only follow Him! You must know His voice and His alone, to successfully navigate in this life.

When my wife Cindy was seven years old, she and some other family members witnessed a tragedy at Magnolia Gardens Park on the San Jacinto River in Houston, Texas. The park wraps around a bend in the river. You can google the park and find advertisements that declare, "It's a great place to bring the family! Come play, B.B.Q. Swim."

On a certain day in 1968, Cindy's oldest sister's first husband, who was a life guard and a strong swimmer, died while attempting to swim across the San Jacinto River. He was almost to the other side when, according to Cindy, an undertow dragged him beneath the water. He kept fighting the downward pull and surfaced once, waving frantically. But the undertow pinned him beneath a log below the river's surface. He never came up again. Everyone looked on, helplessly stunned! I guarantee you that young man didn't get up that morning with the thought that he was about to be swept out into eternity.

It is interesting that we presently live in Walden on Lake Conroe. We have a boat that we keep in a boat slip at Walden Marina. Part of the San Jacinto River was dammed up to form Lake Conroe. That means river currents and undertows are in Lake Conroe, as well. Monitored, sensible swimming is fine in that lake, but it is not wise to try to swim across it.

Whenever I'm in our boat, out on the lake, I like to watch the depth finder. Often the boat will be going along at a certain depth, and then suddenly a drop will occur. It may be a 20 to 30 foot drop-off, or more. A person living at Lake Conroe could wade or swim out a little ways, expecting the water to just gradually get deeper, when suddenly he or she encounters a drop off. The water is unpredictable, so you must be careful.

That's the way these twelve seducing spirits work. They manifest suddenly to catch you by surprise. Their intention is to suck you under and pin you down, so you'll never come up again. Take heed to this course as a warning! Don't be nonchalant about this study!

It's kind of like a James Bond movie: It doesn't matter what actor is playing the part; there is always somebody who appears in the story as Bond's ally, but is either a double agent or an undercover arch enemy. It takes time to flush 'em out.

In the ministry, it can also take a while to flush 'em out, to see who, on your staff or leadership team, is a double agent or an undercover arch enemy. The test of time never fails!

3. The Absalom Spirit

"The Spirit of Jealousy and Conspiracy"

The Absalom spirit affects the family members of the one whom God has chosen to head a ministry. This is a devastating spirit, as it causes the recipient to be consumed with jealousy to the degree that a detailed, calculated plot will emerge, the sole purpose of which is to discredit, overthrow and destroy God's anointed. This spirit will cause you to be part of such a conspiracy against God's leaders.

Let's look at the passage of scripture from which this spirit derives its name: 2 Samuel 15:1-6, which recounts the story of David's son, Absalom:

"As time went on, Absalom took to riding in a horse-drawn chariot, with fifty men running in front of him. Early each morning he would take up his post beside the road at the city gate. When anyone showed up with a case to bring to the king for a decision, Absalom would call him over and say, "Where do you hail from?" And the answer would come, "Your servant is from one of the tribes of Israel."

Then Absalom would say, "Look, you've got a strong case; but the king isn't going to listen to you." Then he'd say, "Why doesn't someone make me a judge for this country? Anybody with a case could bring it to me and I'd settle things fair and square." Whenever someone would treat him with special

> *honor, he'd shrug it off and treat him like an equal, making him feel important. Absalom did this to everyone who came to do business with the king and stole the hearts of everyone in Israel (MSG)."*

This is about as low as a person can get, to construct a plot behind his father's back just to make himself look good. What a conniver Absalom was! He impugned his own father's reputation by questioning David's ability to lead the kingdom. He even embraced and kissed the cheeks of the men with whom he wanted to obtain favor.

Absalom worked on these people, one by one, behind the king's back, until he stole their hearts. The people began to believe Absalom and doubt David. They thought Absalom was sweet and kind, and the king was bold and harsh.

The same thing goes on today. A disloyal family member in leadership can bring great devastation if not dealt with. This person will make statements such as, "This is how I would handle the situation if I were in charge." An Absalom might also say,"He or she is too busy to meet with you, but I'm not." An Absalom will become jealous of the leader's position and popularity. Is there someone serving you in ministry, who is misrepresenting you? Or are you being wooed by an Absalom to take his or her side against God's anointed?

Given enough time, an Absalom will raise an army of people to march against the king, leader, or minister, completely confident of a victory. An Absalom spirit will cause many casualties, including the perpetrator, himself, if true repentance doesn't come. This is made very clear in the case of David's son, Absalom, who got hung up in an oak tree when his mule ran under the branches. While he hung there, helpless, Joab stabbed him to death (2 Sam.18:9,10,14,15, MSG).

My wife Cindy and I experienced the Absalom Spirit, but have since found restoration with that particular family member. I wouldn't wish what we went through on any human being, not even my worst enemy.

A. Characteristics of the Absalom Spirit:

1. You will begin to pass judgment on your own family members.
2. You want to be in charge of everything.
3. You will make statements such as, "I'll tell you what I would do if I were in charge."
4. You will be persuaded that your leader is responsible for his/her situation and that no one else could help in any way.
5. You will be drawn to hang out with those who have been placed under church discipline and those found to be troublemakers.
6. You will draw people together that possess the same kind of problems that you have.
7. The Absalom spirit will cause you to begin to act politic, to kiss cheeks, and put down the head minister.
8. This spirit will cause you to accuse your leader of being too strict, harsh, and untouchable.

9. Last of all, you will march against church leadership to your own demise.

B. The Absalom Test for Leaders:

1. Do I believe that the one whom I serve in the ministry is too hard or too strict?
2. Do I often have the desire to share what bothers me with others?
3. Do I try to get together with individuals who have the same problems that I have?
4. Do I act politic, kiss cheeks, or lick the wounds of people who have hurt feelings and accusations against church leadership?
5. Do I ever think or say, "If I were in charge . . ."?
6. Do I find that I am most at ease when I am around individuals that are disturbed, instead of pure and holy fruit-bearers?

The Absalom Test for Relationships:

1. Do I feel that my spouse or boss is too harsh or strict?
2. Do I find myself sharing the things that bother me with others?
3. Do I spend time with others who have the same problems as I do?
4. Do I side with, and lick the wounds of, those who have hurt feelings or grudges against my boss?
5. Do I ever think (concerning my work environment), "If only I were in charge..."?

6. Do I talk in such a way as to stir up discord at home or in my workplace against those in positions of authority over me?

If you answered yes to any of the above, you need to sincerely repent and turn completely to the Lord for total restoration!

Pray this prayer:

Father, I come to you in the name of Jesus. I ask you to forgive me for yielding myself to an Absalom spirit. Forgive me for tolerating and being sympathetic to Absalom's ways. Purify my heart, Lord. Remove every wicked way from my life. Help me to boldly stand against this destructive thought process. Help me to receive the saving of my soul man (mind, will, and emotions) in this area according to 1 Peter 1:9, which is the end or goal of my faith. Even more specifically, help me receive the saving and delivering of my mind (thoughts, feelings, and affections) in this area. Without reservation, I bind and renounce the Spirit of Absalom. I pull down this stronghold in my life and bring every thought into captivity to the obedience of Christ. You have been found out, Absalom, and will no longer work in my life. Let me walk in Your Light, Lord, and give me discerning eyes and ears to recognize and expose any darkness in my path. I am totally free, and will remain free. I give you praise for this, Father, in Jesus' name, Amen.

4. The Saul Spirit

The Spirit of Religion and Pride

According to 1 Samuel, chapter 9, Saul was chosen by God to be king over Israel. He was a fine, handsome young man. Verse 2 says, "There was none finer—he literally stood head and shoulders above the crowd (The Message)!" He had such a bright future: the anointing of God was upon him and he had available to him the wisdom and blessings of God. But, somewhere along the way, Saul messed up big time!

In 1 Samuel 15, we read that God instructed Saul to take his army and go against Amalek. He was to totally destroy the Amalakites—men, women, children, even the animals. But Saul decided it was okay to spare Agag, king of the Amalekites, and to allow his soldiers to keep some of the choice sheep and cattle to sacrifice to the Lord.

When Samuel heard of this, he confronted King Saul about his disobedience, but Saul did not quite see it the same way:

> *"Saul defended himself. 'What are you talking about? I did obey God. I did the job God set for me. I brought in King Agag and destroyed the Amalekites under the terms of the holy ban. So the soldiers saved back a few choice sheep and cattle from the holy ban for sacrifice to God at Gilgal --what's wrong with that? (1 Sam 15:20-21, MSG)'"*

Check out these facts about Saul:

1. He failed as a leader by disobeying God and caving in to the fear of man. (1 Samuel 15:1-35)
2. Saul allowed jealousy to consume him. (1 Samuel 18:8-9)
3. He attempted murder, by means of a javelin. (1 Samuel 18:11)
4. Saul had priests murdered because they didn't take his side (1 Samuel 22:16-19)
5. An evil religious spirit eventually possessed him. (1 Samuel 16:14, 18:10)
6. Saul's daughter despised unashamed worship to the Lord. (2 Samuel 6:14-16)
7. Saul lashed out at the Prophet Samuel and tore his clothes. (1 Samuel 15:27-28)
8. Saul forever forfeited the kingdom remaining in his lineage by intruding into the priesthood office. (1 Samuel 13:7-14)
9. Saul turned to a witch for assistance. (1 Samuel 28:3-10)
10. Saul committed suicide. (1 Samuel 31:4-6)

1 Samuel 15:27-29 tells us that as Samuel tried to leave, Saul grabbed at the priest's robe and tore it. Samuel said,

> *"God has just now torn the kingdom from you, and handed it over to your neighbor, a better man than you are. Israel's God-of-Glory doesn't deceive and he doesn't dither. He says what he means and means what he says (MSG)."*

The Spirit of Saul will cause a person to lash out at God's anointed when he has lost his own anointing. Because jealousy is not dealt with, it will cause an individual to act religious, put down other ministers, get outside his own assignment, be fueled with a rage that kills others, frame his own loved ones, and run wild on his ministry, like a tyrant out of control.

A. Characteristics of the Spirit of Saul:

1. Always tries to attach itself to God's chosen servants and their family members.
2. This spirit will cause you to turn against your own helpers.
3. You will start to disobey God without even realizing it.
4. You begin to be jealous of the success of other individuals.
5. You will lash out at God's prophets when they correct you.
6. You will get out of your own assignment.
7. You will harm God's mantle and His ministers.
8. You will begin to fear the opinions of other people.

B. The Saul Test for Leaders:

1. Do I become jealous of other Christians or ministries?
2. Do I lash out at my leaders when they correct me?
3. Do I constantly need to be confronted with my sin because I don't see it in time?
4. Do I regularly believe that I could make it quite well with the absence of any spiritual leadership?
5. Do I find there are times when I despise outbursts of worship like shouts, dancing, etc.?
6. Do I view myself more highly than I should?

THE SAUL TEST FOR RELATIONSHIPS:

1. Do I become jealous of family members, friends or co-workers?
2. Do I lash out at family members, friends, co-workers or my boss when they correct me?
3. Am I blind to my own bad behavior, and do I need to be constantly confronted about it by my family members, friends, co-workers or my boss?
4. Do I view myself more highly than I should?

If you answered yes to any of the above, you need to sincerely repent and turn completely to the Lord for total restoration!

Pray this prayer:

Father, I come to you in the name of Jesus. I ask you to forgive me for yielding myself to the Spirit of Saul. Forgive me for tolerating and being sympathetic to Saul's ways. Purify my heart, Lord. Remove every wicked way from my life. Help me to boldly stand against this destructive thought process. Help me to receive the saving of my soul man (mind, will, and emotions) in this area according to 1 Peter 1:9, which is the end or goal of my faith. Even more specifically, help me receive the saving and delivering of my mind (thoughts, feelings, and affections) in this area. Without reservation, I bind and renounce the Spirit of Saul. I pull down this stronghold in my life and bring every thought into captivity to the obedience of Christ. You have been found out, Saul, and will no longer work in my life. Let me walk in Your Light, Lord, and give me discerning eyes and ears to recognize and expose any darkness in my path. I am totally free, and will remain free. I give you praise for this, Father, in Jesus' name, Amen.

5. The Iscariot Spirit

The Spirit of Hidden Betrayal, and Muddled Repentance

Matthew 26:14-16 recounts how Judas betrayed Jesus for money: *"when one of the Twelve, the one named Judas Iscariot, went to the cabal of high priests and said, 'What will you give me if I hand him over to you?' They settled on thirty silver pieces. He began looking for just the right moment to hand him over (MSG)."*

What we are dealing with here is the demonic spirit that drove Judas Iscariot to do what he did. Judas died, but the spirit that enticed him is still working in the earth today. Not only is it in the earth, it is specifically targeting families, churches and ministries.

Judas was one of the chosen twelve, but never appeared to have the same spirit and heart as the other eleven. He questioned what Jesus did, and communicated an attitude of spiritual authority higher than the eleven, and at times, higher than Jesus Himself.

One example of this "sense of spiritual authority" is found in John 12: 1-6, in the account of Jesus' visit to the homes of Mary, Martha and Lazarus. As Jesus sat, visiting with his friends, Mary came in with a jar of aromatic oil that was quite expensive for the days in which they were living. She wasted no time anointing the feet of Jesus with that costly oil and wiping His feet dry with her hair.

Judas saw this act of reverence and asked,

"Why wasn't this oil sold and the money given to the poor? It would have easily brought three hundred silver pieces (John 12:5, MSG)."

Notice how Judas displays a hollow, superficial spirituality by voicing his great concern for the poor. He obviously didn't care for the poor, or he wouldn't have been stealing from the ministry treasury. Yes, stealing! According to the scriptures, Judas was a thief—and a very sneaky one at that.

This spirit will cause people to worry about how the preacher uses the money that is given to the ministry.

It will cause a person to be jealous of the love, appreciation, and money that is given to the man or woman of God. An Iscariot spirit will cause the recipient to question the character and integrity of the minister, whom he or she is serving.

In Matthew, chapter 26, we read the account of the Last Supper, in which Jesus is sharing the Passover meal with his disciples. It was at this time that Jesus told the twelve that one of them would betray Him. Of course, this caused quite a stir among the disciples, as they wondered what Jesus meant—and who this betrayer might be:

"They were exceedingly pained and distressed and deeply hurt and sorrowful and began to say to Him one after another, Surely it cannot be I, Lord, can it?

He replied, He who has [just] dipped his hand in the same dish with Me will betray Me!

The Son of Man is going just as it is written of Him; but woe to that man by whom the Son of Man is betrayed! It would have been better (more profitable and wholesome) for that man if he had never been born! [Psalms 41:9.]

Judas, the betrayer, said, Surely it is not I, is it, Master? He said to him, You have stated [the fact] (Matt. 26:22-25, AMP)."

In Luke, chapter 22, we find a parallel account which shows just how easily this spirit can blend into its surroundings and go unnoticed—even by God's chosen! Despite the fact that Jesus explicitly pointed out Judas as His betrayer, the scripture tells us, "They immediately became suspicious of each other and began quizzing one another, wondering who might be about to do this (Lk.22:23, MSG)."

This deadly demon will enable a person to become an undetectable pretender, imitator and traitor. The other eleven never suspected Judas of being a traitor. In other words, other church or ministry staff won't have a clue.

This demon will enable you to play the part of being a Christian so well that only you—and God-- will know the difference. This demon is running rampant in churches and ministries today.

Let's look at John 13:21-30:

"After he said these things, Jesus became visibly upset, and then he told them why. 'One of you is going to betray me.'

The disciples looked around at one another, wondering who on earth he was talking about. One of the disciples, the one Jesus loved dearly, was reclining against him, his head on his shoulder. Peter motioned to him to ask who Jesus might be talking about. So, being the closest, he said, "Master, who?"

Jesus said, 'The one to whom I give this crust of bread after I've dipped it.' Then he dipped the crust and gave it to Judas, son of Simon the Iscariot. As soon as the bread was in his hand, Satan entered him. 'What you must do,' said Jesus, 'do. Do it and get it over with.'

No one around the supper table knew why he said this to him. Some thought that since Judas was their treasurer, Jesus was telling him to buy what they needed for the Feast, or that he should give something to the poor. Judas, with the piece of bread, left. It was night (MSG)."

Notice that even after Jesus implicated that Judas Iscariot would be the traitor, some of the eleven still didn't catch on; they were confused and disillusioned. This shows how convincing this demon is.

The Spirit of Iscariot will not only take control of the one who yields to it, but will also disillusion and fluster those around it. It is extremely difficult for a leader to expose a traitor, as others may desire to side with, or defect to, the one exposed.

While Judas was with Jesus and under His anointing, he seemed to fit in; but as soon as he entered a different environment, he fit in there as well. A Judas is a chameleon; he can fit in anywhere.

This demon will give a person a dual personality and vocabulary--one when you are around other Christians and another when you are with religious people or the world.

Compromise will become a way of life, as your values will be derived from a polluted stream. You will make all the wrong choices as you forsake "right" and embrace "wrong."

This is a very difficult demonic mindset from which to recover. An Iscariot spirit has been around the most powerful anointed meetings, unfazed and unchanged. That is a dangerous place in which to find oneself. This individual's conscience has become seared, cauterized, beyond feeling. He or she can no longer distinguish right from wrong.

Many never recover from this spirit. Their lives become a trash heap. Judas didn't recover: He committed suicide! People have come to me entertaining the possibility that Judas made it to heaven. No one with knowledge of the scripture would ever consider such a thought. Matthew 26:24 makes this evident: "...that man who turns him in, turns traitor to the Son of Man — better never to have been born than do this! (MSG)"

John 17:12 backs this up. Here, Jesus says of His disciples: "While I was with them in the world, I kept them in Your name. Those whom You gave Me I have kept; and none of them is lost except the son of perdition, that the Scripture might be fulfilled (NKJV)."

It's not good, when Jesus' own commentary about you is that it would have been better for you, had you never been born.

John 18:2-3 tells us that Judas knew where Jesus was going to meet with His disciples the night he betrayed Him. He knew all the meeting places, because he kept close to the other disciples, following them as they followed Jesus.

This spirit will cause you to keep coming to church. You will continue to attend ministerial staff meetings, but all the while you will be plotting the ultimate betrayal.

The Iscariot Spirit will continue to grow stronger in you the more you entertain it. It will cause you to become bold, so bold that you will betray the man or woman of God publicly, even with a kiss.

Matthew 27:3-5 clearly indicates this tendency, as it manifested in Judas Iscariot:

"Judas, the one who betrayed him, realized that Jesus was doomed. Overcome with remorse, he gave back the thirty silver coins to the high priests, saying, 'I've sinned. I've betrayed an innocent man.' They said, 'What do we care? That's your problem!' Judas threw the silver coins into the Temple and left. Then he went out and hung himself (MSG)."

Someone might say, "See, Judas repented." Sure he did, to the people he sinned with, but never to Jesus. Jesus was the One he had sinned against and the only One Who had the power to forgive him.

Repenting to your sinning buddies accomplishes nothing. Only Jesus can forgive sin. Once the sin is forgiven, true repentance will cause you to make the wrong right. However, as in this case, the wrong could never be made right. He sold the Son of God to the killer mob for money.

The final ploy of this demonic spirit is to tempt you to commit suicide.

A. Characteristics of the Iscariot Spirit:

1. This spirit will gradually cause you to possess a dual personality.
2. You will become the ultimate pretender.
3. You will come to the place of betraying your leaders with a kiss.
4. This spirit will bring you to the place in which you even question the integrity of Christ and His Word.
5. You will feel responsible for the individuals whom you deceive.
6. This type of individual is very sneaky. You will come to a place where you trade your relationship with Christ for money.
7. You will have the desire to repent, but to those with whom you sinned, instead of the people you sinned against (and the only one who can remove sin, Jesus Christ.)
8. This demon spirit is closely related to a spirit of suicide.

B. The Iscariot Test for Leaders:

1. Do I ever wonder why other believers always seem to be more committed than I am?
2. Do I find myself acting less Christ-like when I am around those who are lost?

3. Is money of great importance to me?
4. Am I jealous of my pastor or Christian leader, and am I concerned about all the attention he or she gets?
5. Do I allow people to speak against my church, pastor, ministry or minister in front of me; and do I say nothing in their defense?
6. Does anyone in my life really know what I am like in private; and, if so, do I avoid those who do know?
7. Do I often repent to people with whom I sin, instead of those I sin against (when the only person who can remove my sin is Jesus Christ)?
8. Do I ever battle with thoughts of suicide?

THE ISCARIOT TEST FOR RELATIONSHIPS:

1. Do I find myself hanging out with ungodly people at work or on my days off?
2. Do I act less Christ-like at home, at work or at play?
3. Is money more important to me than family or service to God?
4. Am I jealous when my spouse or co-workers get more attention than I do?
5. Do I allow people to say bad things about my spouse, friends, co-workers or boss in front of me, yet I say nothing in their defense?
6. Do my friends, co-workers or boss really know what I am like in private; and do I avoid those who do know "the real me"?

7. Do I ever battle with depression and thoughts of suicide?

If you answered yes to any of the above, you need to sincerely repent and turn completely to the Lord for total restoration!

Pray this prayer:

Father, I come to you in the name of Jesus. I ask you to forgive me for yielding myself to an Iscariot spirit. Forgive me for tolerating and being sympathetic to Iscariot's ways. Purify my heart, Lord. Remove every wicked way from my life. Help me to boldly stand against this destructive thought process. Help me to receive the saving of my soul man (mind, will, and emotions) in this area according to 1 Peter 1:9, which is the end or goal of my faith. Even more specifically, help me receive the saving and delivering of my mind (thoughts, feelings, and affections) in this area. Without reservation, I bind and renounce the Spirit of Iscariot. I pull down this stronghold in my life and bring every thought into captivity to the obedience of Christ. You have been found out, Iscariot, and will no longer work in my life. Let me walk in Your Light, Lord, and give me discerning eyes and ears to recognize and expose any darkness in my path. I am totally free, and will remain free. I give you praise for this, Father, in Jesus' name, Amen.

6. The Ten Spies Spirit

The Contagious Spirit of Doubt, Disbelief and Giving Up

In Deuteronomy 1:21-28, we read the account of the twelve Israelites, who were sent into the Promised Land to scout out the area and bring back a report to Moses and the people, concerning their findings. As you may recall, ten of those spies brought a frightening report: "The people are bigger and stronger than we are; their cities are huge, their defenses massive — we even saw Anakite giants there! (verse 28, MSG)"

Although their initial findings were much more positive—"It's a good land that God, our God, is giving us! (verse 25, MSG)"—they let doubt and fear overwhelm them and prevent them from appropriating God's fullest blessings. Instead of obeying God, the people began to murmur and complain. The Promised Land lay ahead of them, but they wanted to return to Egypt!

This spirit will cause you to doubt God's word, resist the one over you in the Lord, and to turn back to Egypt, a type of bondage. It will cause you to die on the wrong side of the river, devoid of God's promises.

This deadly spirit infected the entire congregation to the degree that anointed faith-filled leadership could not change the people's minds.

This demon will cause you to quit doing anything, and expect God to do it all. There are two aspects of faith that God requires His people to engage in — speaking and action. You can always locate someone by what he or she says and does. Faith is expressed by what you say and do, so is doubt and unbelief.

This demonic influence will convince you that if God wants you to have it, He'll come down here and give it to you.

The Ten Spies Spirit will cause you to have a very small and distorted view and opinion of yourself. These people said that their adversaries viewed them the same way they viewed themselves — as mere grasshoppers. Do you have a grasshopper complex? Do you bring grasshopper reports to the congregation, or do you bring faith-filled reports to God's people?

Don't be the board member who says, "How are we going to do that?" or "Where are we going to get the money?"

Don't die on the wrong side of the river, devoid of God's promises. Wake up! Change!

Let's take a look at two more scriptures:

> 25 *After forty days of scouting out the land, they returned home.* 26 *They presented themselves before Moses and Aaron and the whole congregation of the People of Israel in the Wilderness of Paran at Kadesh. They reported to the whole congregation and showed them the fruit of the land.* 27 *Then*

they told the story of their trip: "We went to the land to which you sent us and, oh! It does flow with milk and honey! Just look at this fruit!
28 The only thing is that the people who live there are fierce, their cities are huge and well fortified. Worse yet, we saw descendants of the giant Anak. 29 Amalekites are spread out in the Negev; Hittites, Jebusites, and Amorites hold the hill country; and the Canaanites are established on the Mediterranean Sea and along the Jordan."
30 Caleb interrupted, called for silence before Moses and said, "Let's go up and take the land — now. We can do it."
31 But the others said, "We can't attack those people; they're way stronger than we are." 32 They spread scary rumors among the People of Israel. They said, "We scouted out the land from one end to the other — it's a land that swallows people whole. Everybody we saw was huge.
33 Why, we even saw the Nephilim giants (the Anak giants come from the Nephilim). Alongside them we felt like grasshoppers. And they looked down on us as if we were grasshoppers (Num 13:25-33 MSG)."

1The whole community was in an uproar, wailing all night long. 2 All the People of Israel grumbled against Moses and Aaron. The entire community was in on it: "Why didn't we die in Egypt? Or in this wilderness? 3 Why has God brought us to this country to kill us? Our wives and children are about to become plunder. Why don't we just head back to Egypt? And right now!" 4 Soon they were all saying it to one another: "Let's pick a new leader; let's head back to Egypt (Num 14:1-4 MSG)."

This spirit will cause you to whine and bellyache, like a two-year-old baby. There comes a time when we must grow up. One reason the church cannot handle any more new converts than she presently has is that the spiritual nursery is full. There are no spare bottles for the new babes in Christ. We need to get off the bottle, quit whining, grow up and start believing God's word.

Just think of it, forty years was added to their current age, and they never stopped doubting, whining and complaining. They never grew up. God had to let them die off to bring in a new generation. Be determined to be that new generation of Calebs and Joshuas.

A. Characteristics of the Ten Spies Spirit:

1. These people were upset that God didn't just hand over their blessings.
2. This group of people was so disappointed that they had to take some action themselves to obtain their blessings.
3. They viewed themselves as grasshoppers.
4. They stirred up the entire congregation.
5. This spirit will hold an individual or a group of people captive with doubt and unbelief instead of faith.
6. This demonic force will cause a person to look at the obstacles he or she is facing, instead of the promises of God.
7. Those who entertain this spirit will remain on the wrong side of the river, never able to walk in the fullness of God's promises and blessings.
8. These people will not only stand against the pastor or spiritual leader, but will rally against him.

B. The Ten Spies Test for Leaders:

1. Are there times when I am convinced that God should simply hand over His blessings to me without requiring anything from me?
2. Am I focused on the obstacles in my way instead of God's ability to enable me to overcome them?
3. Do I find myself stirring up other individuals in order to prove my point?
4. Do I ever rally against my leaders in Christ?
5. Do the giants I am facing look bigger to me than my God?
6. Do I have a poor image of myself, one that is inferior to what the Word says?
7. Am I able to recognize the promises of God, but feel I will never be able to experience the manifestation of them for myself?
8. Do I believe my pastor or spiritual leader is not able to lead me into the Promised Land?

The Ten Spies Test for Relationships:

1. Do I expect God's blessings at home or at work without any effort on my part to obtain those blessings?
2. Do I focus on the obstacles in my way at home or at work, rather than on God's ability to enable me to overcome those obstacles?
3. Do I find myself stirring up family members or co-workers in order to prove my point?
4. Do I ever rally against my boss or those in positions of

authority over me at work?

5. Do the giants in my home life or workplace look bigger to me than my God?
6. Do I struggle with a poor self-image, one that is inferior to what the Word of God says about me?
7. Do I recognize God's promises, but feel they will never manifest in my own life?

If you answered yes to any of the above, you need to sincerely repent and turn completely to the Lord for total restoration!

Pray this prayer:

Father, I come to you in the name of Jesus. I ask you to forgive me for yielding myself to the Ten Spies Spirit. Forgive me for tolerating and being sympathetic to the Ten Spies' ways. Purify my heart, Lord. Remove every wicked way from my life. Help me to boldly stand against this destructive thought process. Help me to receive the saving of my soul man (mind, will, and emotions) in this area according to 1 Peter 1:9, which is the end or goal of my faith. Even more specifically, help me receive the saving and delivering of my mind (thoughts, feelings, and affections) in this area. Without reservation, I bind and renounce the Spirit of the Ten Spies. I pull down this stronghold in my life and bring every thought into captivity to the obedience of Christ. You have been found out, Ten Spies Spirit, and will no longer work in my life. Let me walk in Your Light, Lord, and give me discerning eyes and ears to recognize and expose any darkness in my path. I am totally free, and will remain free. I give you praise for this, Father, in Jesus' name, Amen.

7. The Demas Spirit

"The Spirit of Loving This Present World"

Philemon 24 tells us that the Apostle Paul had four co-workers: Mark, Aristarchus, Demas, and Luke. It appears that Demas was an intricate part of Paul's apostolic team that traveled around the world, preaching the gospel and building the church.

The Apostle Paul certainly had the most prominent ministry during that time, so Demas operated in an elevated spot in the church world as he labored with Paul. But Demas did the unthinkable: he defected!

> *"Make every effort to come to me soon. For Demas has deserted me for love of this present world and has gone to Thessalonica; Crescens [has gone] to Galatia, Titus to Dalmatia (2 Tim 4:9-10 AMP)."*

Not only is it clear from this passage that Demas was no longer with the Apostle Paul, but that he had also left the ministry altogether. What kind of demonic force can successfully entice a man to leave his God-given ministry assignment and go hog-wild back into the cesspool of this world? It is a persistent spirit that is constantly trying various lures to see which one will cause the fish to bite. Jesus told Simon Peter and his brother Andrew to come follow Him, and He would make them fishers of men. Likewise,

Satan has followers that are fishing with a set of hell's lures to entice people to go for Satan's bait which, when taken, will ultimately lead them to hell itself.

Let's take a look at the three things this demon spirit did in the life of Demas. Then we will simultaneously consider a parallel of these three in some church and ministry team members today.

First, Demas deserted the Apostle Paul; he left him high and dry. Leaving your pastor or spiritual leader and going with a stranger on your own initiative is always the telltale sign of spiritual trouble.

Second, Demas entertained Satan's bait until he fell head over heels in love with this world. The correct use of the word love here means that he set his will in that direction in order to find joy in something or someone. He had cast off restraint, and set his affection on the things of this world. The moment you cast off restraint in your life, you are done for. Casting off restraint is a sign you have lost your vision. Growing cold and losing your focus is a sure sign that you have distanced yourself from the visionary God has placed in your life. When this happens, the world looks extremely attractive. You must know that the world's attractions are the believer's distractions.

> *"If people can't see what God is doing, they stumble all over themselves; But when they attend to what he reveals, they are most blessed (Proverbs 29:18 MSG)."*

> *"Where there is no vision the people cast off restraint; but happy is he that keepeth the law (Proverbs 29:18, Darby)."*

Third, Demas left. It is only a matter of time for someone, who has already taken the first two steps, to defect. We must learn from Demas, and keep all doors shut to this demonic influence. Stay full of God's vision for your life, and don't allow anyone or anything to lure you away from the visionary God has placed in your life. Don't let the Demas spirit attach itself to you, and don't hang out with people who have it.

Know this! The world has only three things to offer a person, and none of them are good.

1. The lust of the flesh.
2. The lust of the eyes.
3. The pride of life.

> *"...because all that [is] in the world, the lust of the flesh, and the lust of the eyes, and the pride of life, is not of the Father, but is of the world (1 John 2:16, Darby)."*

A. Characteristics of the Demas Spirit:

1. This demonic force will cause an individual to have his/her eye on the world the whole time he or she is walking with Christ.
2. This person will have a love for the things of this world that will eventually drag him/her back into the world.
3. This person will first forsake the preacher for whom he or she is working.
4. This person will end up leaving the ministry to go out into the world.

5. This spirit's seducing power will actually lead a person to embrace the world that he or she once denounced.

B. The Demas Test for Leaders:

1. Am I pursuing worldly things in place of the things of God?
2. Am I serving in a local church or ministry, but feel put out to a certain extent because of it?
3. Do I feel that God owes me something and that I should be compensated for my services?
4. Does being prosperous only equate to money and possessions in my life?
5. Do I feel the sudden urge to draw away from the local church or ministry in which I am presently serving and go after worldly things?
6. Do I ever feel that my pastor or spiritual leader is hindering or postponing my promotion?
7. Do I, at times, feel that the best thing for me to do is to leave the church and just go for the pleasures, possessions, and promotions of this world?
8. Do I ever become jealous when other people get blessed?

The Demas Test for Relationships:

1. Am I pursuing worldly things, rather than the things of God?
2. Am I struggling to do the best that I can at home or at work,

and feel put out to a certain extent because of it?

3. Does being prosperous only equate to money and possessions in my life?
4. Do I sometimes feel the urge to escape from my family or job and pursue worldly things?
5. Do I ever feel that my boss is hindering or postponing my promotion at work?
6. Do I sometimes feel that I should give up being a godly person at home or at work, and just go for the pleasures, possessions and promotions of the world?
7. Do I ever get jealous when my spouse, family members, friends or co-workers get blessed?

If you answered yes to any of the above, you need to sincerely repent and turn completely to the Lord for total restoration!

Pray this prayer:

Father, I come to you in the name of Jesus. I ask you to forgive me for yielding myself to the Demas Spirit. Forgive me for tolerating and being sympathetic to Demas' ways. Purify my heart, Lord. Remove every wicked way from my life. Help me to boldly stand against this destructive thought process. Help me to receive the saving of my soul man (mind, will, and emotions) in this area according to 1 Peter 1:9, which is the end or goal of my faith. Even more specifically, help me receive the saving and delivering of my mind (thoughts, feelings, and affections) in this area. Without reservation, I bind and renounce the Demas Spirit. I pull down this stronghold in my life and bring every thought into captivity to the obedience of Christ. You have been found out, Demas Spirit, and will no longer work in my life. Let me walk in Your Light, Lord, and give me discerning eyes and ears to recognize and expose any darkness in my path. I am totally free, and will remain free. I give you praise for this, Father, in Jesus' name, Amen.

8. The Gehazi Spirit

"The Spirit of Greed and Selfishness"

In 2 Kings 5:20-27, we read the account of how Gehazi, servant to the prophet Elisha, plotted a way to appropriate for himself a blessing that he felt Elisha had let slip through his fingers.

Naaman, the Aramean general (whom God had cured of leprosy through a word given to Elisha), had just left the prophet and was on his way home. Although Naaman had offered to give Elisha a gift for "services rendered," Elisha would take no payment. But when Gehazi saw this, he thought to himself,

> *"My master has let this Aramean Naaman slip through his fingers without so much as a thank-you. By the living God, I'm going after him to get something or other from him! (verse 20, MSG)"*

Gehazi then concocted a story about two young prophets who just showed up on Elisha's doorstep, needing some money and clothing. He asked Naaman if he could supply them with seventy-five pounds of silver and two changes of clothing. Naaman, thankful for his healing, was more than happy to oblige—and then some!

> *"Naaman said, 'Of course, how about a hundred and fifty pounds?' Naaman insisted. He tied up the money in two sacks and gave him the two sets of clothes; he even gave him two servants to carry the gifts back with him (2 Kings 5:20, MSG)."*

The scriptures tell us that Gehazi stashed the money and clothing in the fort on the hill and sent the servants back to Naaman. He must've felt proud that his little ruse had worked! Or so he thought... But God was about to teach this selfish servant a lesson—one that he would never forget:

> *"He returned and stood before his master. Elisha said, 'So what have you been up to, Gehazi?' 'Nothing much,' he said.*
>
> *Elisha said, 'Didn't you know I was with you in spirit when that man stepped down from his chariot to greet you? Tell me, is this a time to look after yourself, lining your pockets with gifts? Naaman's skin disease will now infect you and your family, with no relief in sight.' Gehazi walked away, his skin flaky and white like snow (2 Kings 5: 25-27, MSG)."*

It's hard for me to understand how a man, like Gehazi, with all the favor and status he experienced, could trade it all for money.

Gehazi just couldn't understand why the prophet Elisha turned down General Naaman's offering for the man of God's services. It bothered Gehazi so much that he became obsessed with getting that offering any way he could. He concocted a story that would persuade the general, then chased Naaman down and delivered the lie. This was a serious transgression. This demon will cause you to lie about what your leader said and to misquote or misrepresent him or her.

General Naaman paid a pretty hefty amount, and the commander's men delivered it to Gehazi's residence. Gehazi then hid the gifts, thinking that the prophet would never know what he had done.

Evidently Gehazi did not know the God that Elisha served. He certainly didn't know him as El Roi, the God Who sees. You can't hide anything from God. Take a look at this verse.

"And not a creature exists that is concealed from His sight, but all things are open and exposed, naked and defenseless to the eyes of Him with Whom we have to do (Hebrews 4:13, AMP)."

It appears Gehazi lost sight of the fact that his boss was a prophet.

And consider this short, but powerful, verse of scripture:

"Surely the Lord God will do nothing without revealing His secret to His servants the prophets (Amos 3:7, AMP)." [see also, Revelation 10:7.]

The Holy Spirit enabled Elisha to see Gehazi's activities in the realm of the spirit. He actually told Gehazi that his spirit went with him and witnessed the sin.

This demon spirit will cause the affected individual to sell out his leader, as well as his own soul. This is a conspiring and lying spirit. This demon is closely related to the Iscariot Spirit.

Look just how far Gehazi fell. He was the assistant to the hands-down, number one ministry on earth at that time. He was next in line to inherit Elisha's mantle, just as Elisha had inherited Elijah's. Instead, he gave it all up to deceive and seek his own personal gain. As a result of his transgression, Gehazi and his seed would never know the absence of the dreaded disease called leprosy, the very one of which General Naaman was healed.

If you permit this demon to affect you, you will also become a selfish, lying deceiver. You will worship money, and will do anything to get it; and any opportunity your spiritual leader turns down will seem like an opportunity for you to step in and be "blessed." You will be completely convinced that this is the only way to get ahead in life, and that God is somehow not moving on your behalf. After all, the prophet turned the blessing down. What harm could there be in appropriating what my leader turned down?

My wife and I learned about the Gehazi Spirit the hard way a number of years ago when we were pastoring. There was a lady serving in the children's ministry who appeared to be the right person for that position. My wife had oversight of the children's ministry and began to suspect something was wrong, but couldn't get a handle on just what it was.

I was teaching about deceitful spirits in an afternoon course at the church at that time. God will always confirm with accompanying signs the part of His word that is being taught. We had no idea that the children's minister was on probation with the law. Reports were being turned in to her probation officer, who lived in another town.

One such report, filed by this children's minister with her probation officer, stated that I, the pastor of the church, allegedly said certain things. This lady forged the name of the pastor of the church for which she said she worked, but it wasn't my name she had written. It was the name of a deceased judge that she signed as the pastor of the church.

The probation officer was Spirit-filled and felt something was wrong with the report, so she called the church and asked to speak to the pastor listed. The secretary told the officer that there was no such pastor, that Darrell McManus was the pastor. She told the officer how to reach me. After speaking to me, the probation officer knew that what she had sensed was true: The children's minister was living a lie. That woman went from being a children's minister to serving jail time very shortly thereafter. Later, we discovered that she was also charging money for parental counseling of a troubled child, without our knowing anything about it. We were so grateful to God for exposing the whole thing.

Remember a Gehazi spirit will always carry and promote a different vision than the head of that particular ministry.

A. Characteristics of the Gehazi Spirit:

1. This demon will cause you to be jealous of the attention that your spiritual leader or pastor gets from people--attention you feel you should get.
2. This demon will persuade you to sneak around the ministry and handle things your own way even though you already know how the pastor has dealt with it.
3. You are willing to conceal things from the Christian leaders in authority in order to be "blessed".
4. You will avail yourself of every opportunity you can, by talking to people on the side and extracting all that you can from them.
5. This demon will drive you to lie to individuals and misrepresent your pastor or Christian leader.

6. This particular spirit will definitely lead you to throw away the future of your entire ministry for the pleasures of today.
7. This demon will persuade you to judge your pastor's or leader's motives.
8. A Gehazi spirit will persuade you to pass judgment on the way your leader or pastor handles people and certain situations.

B. The Gehazi Test for Leaders:

1. Do I ever feel as if my spiritual leader gets all the attention while I do all the work?
2. Am I jealous of the attention that my pastor or leader gets?
3. Do I ever judge how my leader or pastor handles different things, and do I think I could do it better?
4. Do I ever wonder why my Christian leader or pastor turns down business opportunities or certain offerings?
5. Do I try to scavenge everything I can that my pastor or leader turns down (meetings, money, favor with people, position, etc.)?
6. Do I wish I were "the pastor", "the prophet," etc., instead of being satisfied with the assignment that God has given me to complete?
7. Do I live one way in front of my Christian leaders and another way when I am not in their presence?
8. Do I have an ongoing problem with lying?
9. Have I ever lost track of the fact that the Spirit of the Lord and the spirit of the prophet are always with me?

THE GEHAZI TEST FOR RELATIONSHIPS:

1. Do I ever feel that my spouse, family members, friends or co-workers get all the attention while I do all of the work?
2. Am I jealous of the attention that my spouse, family members, friends or co-workers receive?
3. Do I ever judge the way my spouse or family member handles matters at home, or the way my boss handles matters at work; and do I think I could do it better?
4. Do I question why my boss turns down business opportunities?
5. Do I find myself wishing I were in charge at work, rather than being content with my present position and thankful to God for it?
6. Do I act one way in front of my pastor or fellow church members, but another way when I am at home, out with my friends, or at work?
7. Do I have a problem with lying? Do I lie to my family, my friends, my co-workers or my boss?
8. Do I fail to remember that God sees me wherever I am and knows my behavior—even what is "done in darkness"?

If you answered yes to any of the above, you need to sincerely repent and turn completely to the Lord for total restoration!

Pray this prayer:

Father, I come to you in the name of Jesus. I ask you to forgive me for yielding myself to the Gehazi Spirit. Forgive me for tolerating and being sympathetic to Gehazi's ways. Purify my heart, Lord. Remove every wicked way from my life. Help me to boldly stand against this destructive thought process. Help me to receive the saving of my soul man (mind, will, and emotions) in this area according to 1 Peter 1:9, which is the end or goal of my faith. Even more specifically, help me receive the saving and delivering of my mind (thoughts, feelings, and affections) in this area. Without reservation, I bind and renounce the Gehazi Spirit. I pull down this stronghold in my life and bring every thought into captivity to the obedience of Christ. You have been found out, Gehazi Spirit, and will no longer work in my life. Let me walk in Your Light, Lord, and give me discerning eyes and ears to recognize and expose any darkness in my path. I am totally free, and will remain free. I give you praise for this, Father, in Jesus' name, Amen.

9. The Ananias & Sapphira Spirit

"The Spirit of Withholding and Lying to the Holy Spirit"

Let's look, for a moment, at Acts 4:34-5:11. In this passage, we find the account of Ananias and his wife, Sapphira—two believers who made a very bad decision that cost them their lives.

At that time, it was common for believers to pool their resources for the common good: those who had more were willing to share their blessings with those less fortunate, so that "not a person among them was needy, (Acts 4:34, MSG)"

Barnabas, a Levite follower of Christ, sold a field and brought the full selling price as an offering to the apostles. Ananias decided to do likewise, but instead of giving the full selling price to Peter and the apostles, he connived with his wife, Sapphira, to give only a portion and keep the rest for themselves. But, to seem "magnanimous," they opted to lie and say that they were giving the full amount.

When Ananias approached Peter with the money—and the lie—Peter, through the Holy Spirit, knew the truth and called Ananias out on the carpet about it:

> *"Peter said, 'Ananias, how did Satan get you to lie to the Holy Spirit and secretly keep back part of the price of the field? Before you sold it, it was all yours, and after you sold it, the*

> *money was yours to do with as you wished. So what got into you to pull a trick like this? You didn't lie to men but to God (Acts 5:3, 4 MSG).'"*

Upon hearing those words, Ananias fell down dead. His body was removed and buried by the young men of the church. Later, unaware of her husband's fate, Sapphira came in and tried to pull the same stunt on Peter. But Peter confronted her lie, as well:

> *" 'What's going on here that you connived to conspire against the Spirit of the Master? The men who buried your husband are at the door, and you're next.' No sooner were the words out of his mouth then she also fell down, dead. When the young men returned they found her body. They carried her out and buried her beside her husband (Acts 5: 9, 10 MSG)."*

The Bible tells us that these dual deaths brought a "healthy respect" (verse 11, MSG) for God among church members and all who heard of it.

God is restoring a reverential fear of the Lord to His church. Ananias and Sapphira events will surely take place in this hour.

Ananias had a heart full of deceit. He evidently observed how Barnabas had sold a piece of land and sowed the proceeds into the Kingdom. It appears that he wanted to get the attention Barnabas received without the unreserved giving. Remember: God always looks at the heart. You don't know what's deep inside the recesses of a person's heart unless God shows you. God has a special scale that weighs human spirits. All that matters in life is how we measure on that scale.

1 Samuel 16:7 tells us that *"man looks on the outward appearance, but the Lord looks on the heart (AMP)."*

Proverbs 16:2 says, *"All the ways of a man are pure in his own eyes, but the Lord weighs the spirits (the thoughts and intents of the heart) (AMP)." [see also, 1 Samuel 16:7; Hebrews 4:12.]*

And Luke 8:17 reminds us that *"there is nothing hidden that shall not be disclosed, nor anything secret that shall not be known and come out into the open (AMP)."*

Before we go further in this study, we need to take a look at the word grace, because the church needs an accurate understanding of what grace really is. Grace is not being properly taught in many circles. The greater the grace present in the church, the greater the manifested presence and power of the Lord. What you won't find being taught about grace is that five verses before the Ananias and Sapphira event, great grace was upon the church.

Acts 4:33 tells us that the Apostles gave powerful witness of Jesus' resurrection and "great grace was upon them all (Darby)."

Five is God's number for Grace. Not only was great grace mentioned five verses before the judgment, the judgment itself took place in the fifth chapter of Acts. I wonder why this is not being included in the "Grace Message." After all, this is New Testament.

Many of the churches where grace is being taught have no power.

Grace without power is no grace at all.

My definition of grace is unearned and undeserved favor that releases the operational power of God. There is no gospel, whereby an individual can get saved, without the presence of God's power. The power must be present in a tangible way for the new birth to take place.

Romans 1:16 says that the Gospel is *"God's power working unto salvation [for deliverance from eternal death] to everyone who believes with a personal trust and a confident surrender and firm reliance, to the Jew first and also to the Greek (AMP)..."*

What a beautiful—and important—truth!

Paul tells us, in 1 Corinthians 2:1-5, that he didn't come to people with highfalutin speech or cerebral philosophies of men, or even with persuasive "words of wisdom"—but, instead, his preaching was *"in demonstration of the [Holy] Spirit and power [a proof by the Spirit and power of God, operating on me and stirring in the minds of my hearers the most holy emotions and thus persuading them] (verse 4, AMP)."* This was, Paul said, so that their faith (and ours!) would rest solely in the power of God and not the wisdom of men (verse 5).

Grace is a Person! If that Person is not present, there is no Grace. It's just empty words. His name is the Spirit of Grace.

In Hebrews 10:29, we learn that this Spirit of Grace can be offended, if we trample upon the Son of God, cheapening in any way His covenant blood. This act brings "worse punishment (Darby)."

Another important passage of scripture is Hebrews 12:25-29, which says,

> *"See that you do not refuse Him who speaks. For if they did not escape who refused Him who spoke on earth, much more shall we not escape if we turn away from Him who speaks from heaven, whose voice then shook the earth; but now He has promised, saying, "Yet once more I shake not only the earth, but also heaven." Now this, "Yet once more," indicates the removal of those things that are being shaken, as of things that are made, that the things which cannot be shaken may remain. Therefore, since we are receiving a kingdom which cannot be shaken, let us have grace, by which we may serve God acceptably with reverence and godly fear. For our God is a consuming fire (NKJV). "*

I am convinced a number of people who are confessing Jesus as Lord with their mouths are not getting saved. The new birth takes place when two things happen. Those two things are found in Romans 10:9,10:

"that if thou shalt confess with thy mouth Jesus as Lord, and shalt believe in thine heart that God has raised him from among [the] dead, thou shalt be saved. For with [the] heart is believed to righteousness; and with [the] mouth confession made to salvation (Darby)."

Saying with your mouth and agreeing with your head won't get you born again. You must say with your mouth and believe with your heart to get saved. The power of God must be present to believe with the heart. The Gospel is the power of God.

We all know the story, in John chapter 3, about Jesus and the Pharisee, Nicodemus: How Nicodemus came to Jesus at night and expressed his belief that Jesus was a "a teacher come from God; for no one can do these signs that You do unless God is with him. (verse 2, NKJV)." Jesus took that expressed faith and tested it when He replied,

> *"Most assuredly, I say to you, unless one is born again, he cannot see the kingdom of God (verse 3, NKJV)."*

This must have rattled Nicodemas a bit, because he asked right away, *"How can a man be born when he is old? Can he enter a second time into his mother's womb and be born? (vs. 4, NKJV)"*

This is when Jesus laid it all out for Nicodemus:

> *"No doubt about it, Nicodemus," he told the man. "Unless a person is born of both flesh and spirit, he cannot see the kingdom of God. What is born of flesh is flesh; but what is born of spirit is spirit. So, don't marvel if I tell you that you must be born again (vs. 5, NKJV)."*

Ephesians 2:8-10 reminds us that we are saved by grace, through faith, which comes from God and not ourselves. The very faith that we have is a gift from God! This, the scripture tells us, is so that no one can boast about how great his or her faith is.

2 Corinthians 5:17 says,

> *"Therefore, if anyone is in Christ, he is a new creation; old things have passed away; behold, all things have become new (NKJV)."*

Let's look for a moment at another important verse of scripture:

> *"However, I am telling you nothing but the truth when I say it is profitable (good, expedient, advantageous) for you that I go away. Because if I do not go away, the Comforter (Counselor, Helper, Advocate, Intercessor, Strengthener, Standby) will not come to you [into close fellowship with you]; but if I go away, I will send Him to you [to be in close fellowship with you].*
> *And when He comes, He will convict and convince the world and bring demonstration to it about sin and about righteousness (uprightness of heart and right standing with God) and about judgment:*
> *About sin, because they do not believe in Me [trust in, rely on, and adhere to Me] (John 16:7-9 AMP);"*

Since Grace is a person, the Holy Spirit or the Spirit of Grace must be present to be saved by grace. If He is not present, it's just dead words. That is why many times there is no change. A confession without the power of God is a dead confession.

"Yes," you might say, "But didn't God create the moon, the stars and everything else, bringing them into existence by the spoken word?" And I say, no! God never uttered a word until the Holy Spirit was moving. God only spoke when His power was in operation.

The proof of this is found in the first chapter of Genesis, where we learn that the Spirit of God was "moving (hovering, brooding) over the face of the waters. And God said, Let there be light; and there was light (AMP)." God did not speak anything into creation until the Spirit was already moving!

When God told the apostle Paul (concerning the thorn in his flesh) that His grace was sufficient, He was speaking of His operational power. Paul had God's favor to release His power in the situation. He just needed to be reminded of that:

> *"And He said to me, "My grace is sufficient for you, for My strength is made perfect in weakness." Therefore most gladly I will rather boast in my infirmities, that the power of Christ may rest upon me (2 Cor. 12:9, NKJV). "*

Now back to Ananias and Sapphira: This deceptive demon influenced Sapphira to be an accomplice to her husband, Ananias.

The gift of the word of knowledge revealed to the apostle Peter the lie that was being lived out. There was nothing wrong with Ananias selling the land and keeping some or all of the money. What was wrong was that he brought part of the money to the apostles with the impression that he had brought all of it. The presence of the Holy Spirit, the Spirit of Grace, caused the lie to be exposed. Lying to Father God or Jesus without repenting will not bring as swift a judgment as lying to the Holy Spirit will.

The Holy Spirit must be wooed to come into a meeting, but once He is there, the very power source of God is present. If you stay on the right side of electricity, it will bless you. Likewise, you can get on the wrong side of it, and it will kill you.

When God's presence and power are manifested, we must honor, respect and reverentially fear Him. You certainly don't want to test Him by lying to Him to see if the man or woman of God picks up on it. God knows everything!

This type of judgment is actually a manifestation of the working of miracles. Ananias died immediately and the youth ministry that day was to take him out and bury him. What's wrong with our youth today is that they are being entertained but are strangers to God's power. When you experience God's almighty presence and power, what kind of lure can the weaker dark side offer you?

The mercy of God is astounding. When Sapphira came in, about three hours later, the Lord gave her a chance to come clean, but she didn't.

She also dropped dead, and the youth ministry continued with another burial right beside her husband. Did this dampen the church? Absolutely not! Just look at these verses:

> *"So great fear came upon all the church and upon all who heard these things. And through the hands of the apostles many signs and wonders were done among the people. And they were all with one accord in Solomon's Porch. Yet none of the rest dared join them, but the people esteemed them highly. And believers were increasingly added to the Lord, multitudes of both men and women, so that they brought the sick out into the streets and laid them on beds and couches, that at least the shadow of Peter passing by might fall on some of them. Also a multitude gathered from the surrounding cities to Jerusalem, bringing sick people and those who were tormented by unclean spirits, and they were all healed (Acts 5:11-16, NKJV)."*

A. Characteristics of the Ananias and Sapphira Spirit:

1. This demon will cause you to hold back a little for your own self.
2. This spirit will persuade you to lie to your pastors or those over you in the Lord, and ultimately will lead you to lie to the Holy Spirit.
3. This demon will persuade you to go back on your verbal promises to the Lord.
4. You will desire to do right but will consistently give in to cheating somebody, somewhere.
5. You will even think it is all right to break your promise to the preacher and the local church you attend, or the one you just left.
6. This demon desires to eventually persuade you to blaspheme the Holy Spirit.
7. This demon will suck your entire family into these activities and cause them to end up paying the price along with you.

B. The Ananias and Sapphira Test for Leaders:

1. Do I hold back something for myself that I promised to God?
2. Do I keep only part of my promises and pledges made to God and the church I attend or the ministry of which I am a part?
3. Do I ever think it is all right with God to treat my pastor or anyone else in spiritual authority with disrespect?
4. Do I ever feel as if I've gotten away with doing part of

what I was supposed to do, instead of doing all that I was supposed to do?

5. Do I ever involve my family members in my own wrongdoings?
6. Do I act one way in church or pretend that I am in good standing, when I know in my heart that I am not?
7. Has this demon spirit already persuaded me to do things that I've neither repented of nor repaired yet?
8. Do I willingly become involved in activities I know are wrong?

The Ananias and Sapphira Test for Relationships:

1. Do I ever think it is right in the sight of God to disrespect my spouse, family members, friends, co-workers or my boss?
2. Do I ever feel, at home or at work, as if I have gotten away with doing only part of what I was supposed to do, instead of all that I was supposed to do?
3. Do I ever involve family members, friends or co-workers in my own wrongdoings?
4. Do I act "spiritual" in church, as if I am in good standing with the Lord, when I know in my heart that I am not?
5. Has this demon spirit already persuaded me to do things at home or at work for which I've neither repented yet, nor repaired?
6. Am I one who willingly becomes involved in activities with my spouse, co-worker, etc. that I know are wrong?

If you answered yes to any of the above, you need to sincerely repent and turn completely to the Lord for total restoration!

Pray this prayer:

Father, I come to you in the name of Jesus. I ask you to forgive me for yielding myself to the Ananias and Sapphira Spirit. Forgive me for tolerating and being sympathetic to Ananias and Sapphira's ways. Purify my heart, Lord. Remove every wicked way from my life. Help me to boldly stand against this destructive thought process. Help me to receive the saving of my soul man (mind, will, and emotions) in this area according to 1 Peter 1:9, which is the end or goal of my faith. Even more specifically, help me receive the saving and delivering of my mind (thoughts, feelings, and affections) in this area. Without reservation, I bind and renounce the Ananias and Sapphira Spirit. I pull down this stronghold in my life and bring every thought into captivity to the obedience of Christ. You have been found out, Ananias and Sapphira Spirit, and will no longer work in my life. Let me walk in Your Light, Lord, and give me discerning eyes and ears to recognize and expose any darkness in my path. I am totally free, and will remain free. I give you praise for this, Father, in Jesus' name, Amen.

10. The Rich Young Ruler Spirit

The Spirit of Being Curious but Not Hungry

There are three gospel accounts of the story of the rich young ruler in scripture: Matt 19:16-22, Mark 10:17-22 and Luke 18:18-24. Each account details how this young "man of means" stopped Jesus one day and asked Him, *"Teacher, what good thing must I do to get eternal life? (Matt. 19:16, MSG)"*

Jesus, knowing this young man's heart, explained the basics: Don't murder anyone; don't commit adultery; don't lie or steal; honor your parents and love your neighbors.

The young man was quick to affirm that he had kept these commandments all of his life. Mark 10:21 (The Message) says that

> *"Jesus looked him hard in the eye — and loved him!" He knew this youngster had, basically, a good heart, and wanted to do what was right. But there was one thing in his life that held him back—and Jesus knew it!*
>
> *"'If you want to give it all you've got,' Jesus replied, 'go sell your possessions; give everything to the poor. All your wealth will then be in heaven. Then come follow me.' That was the last thing the young man expected to hear. And so, crestfallen, he walked away. He was holding on tight to a lot of things, and he couldn't bear to let go (Matt. 19:21, 22 MSG)."*

The young man was gripped by the things of this world; namely, his material possessions...and he couldn't let go of them, not even to follow Jesus! Is it any wonder that Jesus proclaimed, *"Do you have any idea how difficult it is for people who have it all to enter God's kingdom? (Luke 18:24 MSG)"*

There are three interesting things about this man. He was rich; he had abundant material wealth. He was young; this man had most of his life in front of him. And he was a ruler; he was in a position of authority.

The rich young ruler was curious enough to pursue Jesus, but not hungry enough to receive Him and His kingdom. He knew what it would cost him to follow Christ, but was unwilling to sell out and follow Him. There are many like this today; they seem very interested in the things of God, but it's just cheap talk.

Notice that this man had morals. He knew how to treat his fellow man. He was not a hardened criminal; he was basically a good guy. He was religious, church going. There will be many religious, moral, church going people in hell, because none of the above will get you into heaven. You must be born again to enter the kingdom of God.

People like this are unwilling to give up "the god with a little g" that they are serving. This man's god was money. And according to Matthew 6:24, you cannot serve two masters. This truth is also stated in the gospel of Luke, where we find, *"No servant is able to serve two masters; for either he will hate the one and love the other, or he will stand by and be devoted to the one and despise the other.*

You cannot serve God and mammon (riches, or anything in which you trust and on which you rely) (verse 13, AMP).”

God is truly a jealous God; one of His names is Jealous, according to Exodus 34:14: “(for you shall worship no other god, for the LORD, whose name is Jealous, is a jealous God), (NKJV)”

This “Rich Young Ruler Spirit” is a deceptive demon that will lead you to believe that you can work your way into heaven. It will convince you that the few religious rules you are keeping are enough to make it in. This spirit will tell you that you can serve God in any way you desire.

Any person really hungry for God will gladly lay down money or anything else that would stand in the way of eternal life. It is gross error to believe you can go to heaven without following Christ.

Acts 4:12 states that salvation is found in no one besides Jesus; that His is the only name with the power to save souls. And 1 Timothy 2: 5-6 tells us that Jesus is the only Mediator between God and man: there simply is no other! Jesus Himself declared,

> *“If anyone desires to come after Me, let him deny himself, and take up his cross daily, and follow Me. For whoever desires to save his life will lose it, but whoever loses his life for My sake will save it. For what profit is it to a man if he gains the whole world, and is himself destroyed or lost? For whoever is ashamed of Me and My words, of him the Son of Man will be ashamed when He comes in His own glory, and in His Father’s, and of the holy angels (Luke 9:23-26, NKJV).”*

Jesus also warned us that if we deny Him before men, He will deny us before the Father in heaven (Matt.10:33; Luke 12:9).

The other disciples forsook all and followed Christ. The Rich Young Ruler wanted to keep what he had, and add Christ to the list.

A. Characteristics of the Rich Young Ruler Spirit:

1. This demonic spirit will persuade you to be influenced by money and possessions.
2. This demon will persuade you to loosen your hold on the things of God while strengthening your grip on the prosperity of this world.
3. It will lead you to the place where you are more than willing to let go of your church ministry for overtime on the job.
4. You will be ready to relocate to a different region for a better-paying job, although you are not even sure if there is a good church in that region for your family.
5. It will get you upset when the pastor or minister receives large offerings and asks you to assist financially.
6. This demon spirit will cause you to leave your post in the kingdom of God for recreation or a vacation.
7. This spirit will persuade an individual to dilute God's prosperity to mere financial possessions.
8. This evil spirit will eventually draw you away from serving God and cause you to sink into the world of greed and self-promotion.

B. The Rich Young Ruler Test for Leaders:

1. Does prosperity only mean material gain to me?
2. Am I willing to sacrifice my church worship times for my job?
3. Am I willing to move to a different location for job security, even before I seek out a new church in that part of the country?
4. Am I ever worried, fretful, and fearful that I am giving way too much to the work of the Lord?
5. Am I afraid that serving Jesus is going to cost me everything?
6. Is my job and income more important to me than my outcome?
7. Do I let getting close to God take a back seat in my family to getting ahead in this life?
8. Are my hobbies, crafts, and sports luring me away from God's house more than occasionally?

THE RICH YOUNG RULER TEST FOR RELATIONSHIPS:

1. Does prosperity only mean material gain to me?
2. Am I willing to sacrifice my spouse and/or children for my job?
3. Am I willing to uproot my family and move to a different location for job security, before seeking out a new church in that location?
4. Is my job and income more important to me than my family?
5. Would I rather "get ahead" in life financially than set a

positive, godly example for my spouse and children, or before my friends and co-workers?

6. Are my leisure activities taking me away from my spouse and children?

If you answered yes to any of the above, you need to sincerely repent and turn completely to the Lord for total restoration!

Pray this prayer:

Father, I come to you in the name of Jesus. I ask you to forgive me for yielding myself to the Rich Young Ruler Spirit. Forgive me for tolerating and being sympathetic to the Rich Young Ruler's ways. Purify my heart, Lord. Remove every wicked way from my life. Help me to boldly stand against this destructive thought process. Help me to receive the saving of my soul man (mind, will, and emotions) in this area according to 1 Peter 1:9, which is the end or goal of my faith. Even more specifically, help me receive the saving and delivering of my mind (thoughts, feelings, and affections) in this area. Without reservation, I bind and renounce the Rich Young Ruler Spirit. I pull down this stronghold in my life and bring every thought into captivity to the obedience of Christ. You have been found out, Rich Young Ruler Spirit, and will no longer work in my life. Let me walk in Your Light, Lord, and give me discerning eyes and ears to recognize and expose any darkness in my path. I am totally free, and will remain free. I give you praise for this, Father, in Jesus' name, Amen.

11. The Alexander Spirit

"The Malicious, Defamatory, Intrusive Spirit"

The passage in 1 Tim 1:19-20 tells the story of Hymenaeus and Alexander, two men who *"made shipwreck of their faith (verse 19, AMP)"* and began to harass and trouble Paul—to the point that Paul *"delivered [them] to Satan in order that they may be disciplined [by punishment and learn] not to blaspheme (verse 20, AMP)."* Paul goes on, in 2 Tim. 4:14-15 to warn Timothy, *"Watch out for Alexander the coppersmith. Fiercely opposed to our Message, he caused no end of trouble. God will give him what he's got coming (MSG)."*

When this demon gets in an individual, you will have to publicly mark him or her. The Alexander Spirit will do much harm to an anointed ministry or church. Paul said the Lord reward him for what he has done.

This person will resist the man or woman of God and withstand God's anointed. This is much stronger than simply disagreeing; the Love walk will cause you to disagree agreeably.

Notice, if you will, that Alexander found someone named Hymenaeus, who shared his sentiment. The saying "Misery Loves Company" is applicable here. Sin will always take a person farther than he or she wants to go. This demon will cause you to stand against spiritual authority, take somebody with you, shipwreck your faith, and lose everything.

We live in an anti-authority society. God Himself established authority, so to stand against authority is to stand against God. I understand there is actually exit counseling available to instruct people how to get free from church. It seems obvious to me that these anti-church, anti-five-fold ministry, so-called Christians yelling, "I'm being taken advantage of" or "I'm being controlled" are actually under the control of the Alexander Spirit.

A. Characteristics of the Alexander Spirit:

1. This demonic spirit will turn you completely against spiritual leaders.
2. This demon will have you convinced that Christian leaders are your problem.
3. This spirit will not only persuade you to betray your pastor and local body of believers, but will coerce you to do it maliciously.
4. This evil spirit will drive you to cause extreme damage to the kingdom of God and those in it, while all the while believing you are doing God a service.
5. This demon will lead you to attempt to split the church and slander the ministers.
6. This individual will do the kingdom of God much harm, and much of it will be beyond repair.
7. This demon will eventually persuade you to assault the church and its leaders to the point of bringing your own self under much condemnation.

B. THE ALEXANDER TEST FOR LEADERS:

1. Do I ever entertain the thought that God gave me permission to speak against my brothers and sisters in the Lord?

2. Do I ever feel like I'm the only one in the entire congregation who is right?

3. Do I ever try to persuade other individuals in the church that I'm the one who is right?

4. Do I viciously slander my Christian leaders?

5. Do I ever initiate any action that would lead anybody to leave their church or bring accusations against leadership?

6. Do I ever head up or attend home fellowships or Bible studies that spend their time running down or disassembling other ministries in any way?

7. Am I angry or resentful because I believe that Christians have wronged me, or that pastors are responsible for my activities and misbehavior?

THE ALEXANDER TEST FOR RELATIONSHIPS:

1. Do I ever feel that God has given me the right to speak against my spouse, family members, friends, co-workers or my boss?

2. Do I ever feel, at home or at work, that I am the only one who is right?

3. Do I ever try to persuade family members, friends, co-workers or my boss that I am the one who is right?

4. Do I viciously slander my co-workers or my boss?

5. Do I initiate any action that would cause any of my co-workers to leave the workplace or bring accusations against our boss?
6. Do I ever head up or attend any meetings or gatherings that spend their time running down people in authority, like leaders or bosses?
7. Am I angry or resentful because I feel that my boss or those in authority over me at work have wronged me in some way, or are responsible for my mistakes at work?
8. Am I angry or resentful toward my spouse because I feel that he/she has wronged me in some way and is responsible for my activities or misbehavior?

If you answered yes to any of the above, you need to sincerely repent and turn completely to the Lord for total restoration!!!!!

Pray this prayer:

Father, I come to you in the name of Jesus. I ask you to forgive me for yielding myself to the Alexander Spirit. Forgive me for tolerating and being sympathetic to Alexander's ways. Purify my heart, Lord. Remove every wicked way from my life. Help me to boldly stand against this destructive thought process. Help me to receive the saving of my soul man (mind, will, and emotions) in this area according to 1 Peter 1:9, which is the end or goal of my faith. Even more specifically, help me receive the saving and delivering of my mind (thoughts, feelings, and affections) in this area. Without reservation, I bind and renounce the Alexander Spirit. I pull down this stronghold in my life and bring every thought into captivity to the obedience of Christ. You have been found out, Alexander Spirit, and will no longer work in my life. Let me walk in Your Light, Lord, and give me discerning eyes and ears to recognize and expose any darkness in my path. I am totally free, and will remain free. I give you praise for this, Father, in Jesus' name, Amen.

12. The Diotrephes Spirit

The Bossy, Malicious, Gossiping Spirit of Rejection

In 3 John 9-11, we find the account of a real trouble-maker in the church—a fellow named Diotrephes, who, John declared, "*likes to take the lead among them and put himself first, does not acknowledge my authority and refuses to accept my suggestions or to listen to me (verse 9, AMP).*" This man quite obviously had a "big head" and loved the limelight! He thought he knew best how to run things in the local church and wouldn't even acknowledge the God-ordained authority of the apostle John!

Besides that, Diotrephes had a problem with missionaries. John told Gaius the Elder,

> "*So when I arrive, I will call attention to what he is doing, his boiling over and casting malicious reflections upon us with insinuating language. And not satisfied with that, he refuses to receive and welcome the [missionary] brethren himself, and also interferes with and forbids those who would welcome them, and tries to expel (excommunicate) them from the church (verse 10, AMP).*"

This demonic spirit will seek to undermine spiritual authority when the person in charge is away. Diotrephes will always seek to become the congregation boss. We must always remember that

Satan hates spiritual authority.

Let's take a look at how Diotrephes operates:

First, this demon will come at God's servants with a spirit of rejection. This is to try to undermine the reality of Ephesians 1:3-6:

> *"Blessed be the God and Father of our Lord Jesus Christ, who has blessed us with every spiritual blessing in the heavenly places in Christ, just as He chose us in Him before the foundation of the world, that we should be holy and without blame before Him in love, having predestined us to adoption as sons by Jesus Christ to Himself, according to the good pleasure of His will, to the praise of the glory of His grace, by which He made us accepted in the Beloved (NKJV)."*

Rejection is the opposite of acceptance!

Why did Diotrephes reject the apostle John and his letter to the church? Good question! It appears that John was the only one standing in the way of Diotrephes becoming the sole dictator of that particular church. Dictatorship is the unauthorized usurping of authority.

When Jesus Christ is the Lord of someone's life, he or she will never disregard spiritual authority. Rejecting the person God has placed in charge is a sign of two deep-seated problems: haughtiness and narcissism – two of Satan's chief ploys.

Second, once a person is self-absorbed, he or she will lie to any degree to remain the center of attention. Notice how Diotrephes made malicious and unfounded accusations against God's chosen apostle. He was guilty of the majority of the things God hates in Proverbs, chapter six:

"A proud look [the spirit that makes one overestimate himself and underestimate others], a lying tongue, and hands that shed innocent blood, [see Psalms 120:2,3.], A heart that manufactures wicked thoughts and plans, feet that are swift in running to evil, A false witness who breathes out lies [even under oath], and he who sows discord among his brethren (Prov.6:16-19, AMP)."

And finally, the Diotrephes spirit seeks to obtain total control of the church body or ministerial staff of which he or she is a part. This demonic influence went so far as to stop receiving missionaries in that church.

He threatens to excommunicate any person who tries to receive the missionaries. People seeking control are invariably out of control in their personal lives.

It is important for God-called ministers to stay in the secret place with the Lord and to have God-called intercessors to intercede for them, so a Diotrephes or any of the other seducing spirits will be exposed.

Luke 12:2-3 states this clearly:

"You can't keep your true self hidden forever; before long you'll be exposed. You can't hide behind a religious mask forever; sooner or later the mask will slip and your true face will be known. You can't whisper one thing in private and preach

the opposite in public; the day's coming when those whispers will be repeated all over town (MSG)."

A. Characteristics of the Diotrephes Spirit:

1. This demonic spirit will cause you to become completely self-absorbed.
2. This demon will cause you to become inflated with pride.
3. This spirit will not only persuade you to stand against spiritual authority, but will coerce you to do it maliciously.
4. This evil spirit will drive you to cause extreme damage to the kingdom of God and those in it, all the while believing you are in the right.
5. This demon will persuade you to reject all orders from those over you in the Lord.
6. This individual will lie about God's leaders.
7. Left unchecked, this spirit will take control of the entire congregation or ministry.

B. The Diotrephes Test for Leaders:

1. Do I ever desire to be in charge of the church or ministry in which I'm currently serving?
2. Do I have a hard time receiving and carrying out orders?
3. Does life revolve around me?
4. Will I lie to get ahead?
5. Do I have a problem with missions, missionaries, or missionary offerings?

6. Do I ever want to kick somebody out of the church or ministry in which I serve?
7. Do I believe I'm better than everyone else in the ministry or church in which I presently serve?
8. Do I have to be in charge to be happy?

THE DIOTREPHES TEST FOR RELATIONSHIPS:

1. Do I ever desire to be "in charge" at home, at play, or at work?
2. Do I have a hard time receiving and carrying out orders at work?
3. Do I feel that life should revolve around me?
4. Do I ever lie to my family, friends, or people at work, just to get ahead?
5. Do I ever want to kick somebody out of my place of employment—to get them fired, perhaps?
6. Do I believe I am better than my spouse, family members, friends, co-workers, or even my boss?
7. Do I have to be "in charge" all the time in order to be happy?

If you answered yes to any of the above, you need to sincerely repent and turn completely to the Lord for total restoration!

Pray this prayer:

Father, I come to you in the name of Jesus. I ask you to forgive me for yielding myself to the Diotrephes Spirit. Forgive me for tolerating and being sympathetic to Diotrephes' ways. Purify my heart, Lord. Remove every wicked way from my life. Help me to boldly stand against this destructive thought process. Help me to receive the saving of my soul man (mind, will, and emotions) in this area according to 1 Peter 1:9, which is the end or goal of my faith. Even more specifically, help me receive the saving and delivering of my mind (thoughts, feelings, and affections) in this area. Without reservation, I bind and renounce the Diotrephes Spirit. I pull down this stronghold in my life and bring every thought into captivity to the obedience of Christ. You have been found out, Diotrephes Spirit, and will no longer work in my life. Let me walk in Your Light, Lord, and give me discerning eyes and ears to recognize and expose any darkness in my path. I am totally free, and will remain free. I give you praise for this, Father, in Jesus' name, Amen.

13. Conclusion

As we have seen, the demonic spirits presented in this study are dangerous and destructive. They do their master's work, and they are very good at it, too. It is up to us, as believers, to be on guard against them, so that we do not fall into sin and corruption and, thus, bring dishonor to the Lord. We need to pay heed to the admonition found in 1 Peter 5:8: "Be vigilant, watch. Your adversary [the] devil as a roaring lion walks about seeking whom he may devour (Darby)."

Ephesians 6:11-18:

11 Put on God's whole armor [the armor of a heavy-armed soldier which God supplies], that you may be able successfully to stand up against [all] the strategies and the deceits of the devil.

12 For we are not wrestling with flesh and blood [contending only with physical opponents], but against the despotisms, against the powers, against [the master spirits who are] the world rulers of this present darkness, against the spirit forces of wickedness in the heavenly (supernatural) sphere.

13 Therefore put on God's complete armor, that you may be able to resist and stand your ground on the evil day [of danger], and, having done all [the crisis demands], to stand [firmly in your place].

14 Stand therefore [hold your ground], having tightened the belt of truth around your loins and having put on the breastplate of integrity and of moral rectitude and right

standing with God,
15 And having shod your feet in preparation [to face the enemy with the firm-footed stability, the promptness, and the readiness produced by the good news] of the Gospel of peace.
16 Lift up over all the [covering] shield of saving faith, upon which you can quench all the flaming missiles of the wicked [one].
17 And take the helmet of salvation and the sword that the Spirit wields, which is the Word of God.
18 Pray at all times (on every occasion, in every season) in the Spirit, with all [manner of] prayer and entreaty. To that end keep alert and watch with strong purpose and perseverance, interceding in behalf of all the saints (God's consecrated people). —AMP

May you walk each day fully clothed in the Armor of God, ready and able to deflect all the fiery darts of the enemy that may come against you.

Ephesians 5:15-17:

WALK IN WISDOM

15 See then that you walk circumspectly, not as fools but as wise, 16 redeeming the time, because the days are evil.
17 Therefore do not be unwise, but understand what the will of the Lord is. —NKJV

And remember, as your Father in heaven loves you, walk in Love:

Colossians 3:12-14

12-14 So, chosen by God for this new life of love, dress in the

> *wardrobe God picked out for you: compassion, kindness, humility, quiet strength, discipline. Be even-tempered, content with second place, quick to forgive an offense. Forgive as quickly and completely as the Master forgave you. And regardless of what else you put on, wear love. It's your basic, all-purpose garment. Never be without it.* —MSG

As we take heed to the admonitions given by these scriptures, God will enable us to close any doors of access the enemy may find open in our lives. The following are five doors of access you must always keep shut:

- Discouragement
- Division
- Distractions
- Dissatisfaction
- Disloyalty

My advice is to keep all these doors shut, and throw away the keys!

May God bless you as you serve Him!

Printed in the USA
CPSIA information can be obtained
at www.ICGtesting.com
LVHW080942100124
768241LV00084B/3704

9 781734 527360